W9-BSW-696

SWAHILI
PHRASEBOOK

Martin Benjamin

Charles Mironko

Anne Geoghegan

Swahili phrasebook
2nd edition – July 1998

Published by
Lonely Planet Publications Pty Ltd ABN 36 005 607 983
90 Maribyrnong St, Footscray, Victoria 3011, Australia

Lonely Planet Offices
Australia Locked Bag 1, Footscray, Victoria 3011
USA 150 Linden St, Oakland CA 94607
UK 72-82 Rosebery Ave, London, EC1R 4RW
France 1 rue du Dahomey, 75011 Paris

Cover illustration
Dancing in the Street by Penelope Richardson

ISBN 0 86442 509 0

text © Lonely Planet Publications Pty Ltd 1998
cover illustration © Lonely Planet Publications Pty Ltd 1998

 9 8 7 6 5 4 3   1

Printed through Colorcraft Ltd, Hong Kong
Printed in China

All rights reserved. No part of this publication may be reproduced, stored in a retrieval system or transmitted in any form by any means, electronic, mechanical, photocopying, recording or otherwise, except brief extracts for the purpose of review, without the written permission of the publisher.

Lonely Planet does not allow its name or logo to be appropriated by commercial establishments, such as retailers, restaurants or hotels. Please let us know of any misuses: www.lonelyplanet.com/ip

Lonely Planet and the Lonely Planet logo are trade marks of Lonely Planet and are registered in the U.S. Patent and Trademark Office and in other countries.

Although the authors and Lonely Planet have taken all reasonable care in preparing this book, we make no warranty about the accuracy or completeness of its content and, to the maximum extent permitted, disclaim all liability arising from its use.

About the Authors

Martin Benjamin is the founder and general editor of the *Internet Living Swahili Dictionary* project. His extensive field research in Tanzania for a PhD in Anthropology at Yale University, Connecticut, resulted in a dissertation entitled 'Development Consumers: An Ethnography of "The Poorest of the Poor" and International Aid in Rural Tanzania'.

Charles Mironko is completing a PhD in Anthropology at Yale about the politics of language and ethnicity in Rwanda. He has studied in Zaire, Tanzania and England, and has taught in Burundi, Zaire and Cambodia. He is a co-editor of the *Internet Living Swahili Dictionary*.

Anne Geoghegan has studied in Kenya and Tanzania, and worked in Dar es Salaam. She received her Masters degree from Yale Center for International and Area Studies in their African program in 1996. She has also served as a co-editor on the *Internet Living Swahili Dictionary*.

From the Authors

We take special pleasure in preparing this phrasebook. Together we have worked for several years as editors of the *Internet Living Swahili Dictionary*, an on-going project aimed at producing comprehensive, up-to-date Swahili teaching materials. The latest version of the dictionary can be downloaded for free at http://www.yale.edu/swahili (printouts make great gifts for East African secondary schools!). The dictionary project has brought us into contact with scholars and students of Swahili around the world.

This phrasebook offers us the chance to introduce the pleasure of communicating in Swahili to a new group, people with little or no prior exposure to East Africa. We have tried to imagine situations in which first-time visitors might find themselves, and to employ the most simple yet accurate speech for those situations.

Kiswahili ni kingi, 'there are many ways to speak Swahili' – so it's impossible that this book will meet every need in every place where Swahili is spoken. If there are areas where we have fallen short, or if you have other comments, please let us know. We hope the book will contribute to your enjoyment of your time in East Africa.

There are many people in Tanzania, Kenya, R.D. Congo, Rwanda, and Burundi who have welcomed us into their homes as students and as friends. We would like to dedicate this book to them for the kindness and generosity they have extended to us over the years. We hope these pages adequately reflect their patient teaching.

Thanks also go to the people of Malangali, who have welcomed us as friends and visitors, to the Institute of Swahili Research at the University of Dar es Salaam, to Bi Asia and the rest of the teaching staff at the Foreign Language Institute on Zanzibar, and special thanks to Ann Biersteker for her teaching and guidance.

From the Publisher

This edition is the result of a coordinated effort from a dedicated bunch of authors, editors, artists and designers. It was produced from an original manuscript by Martin Benjamin, Charles Mironko and Anne Geoghegan. Martin was ever-generous with his precious time in helping deliver the book into the world. Quentin Frayne whiled away many hours in the editing suite and racked his brain to create a user-friendly grammar section – his book, *What Noun Class is That?* is in the pipeline! He was ably assisted by Sally Steward and Peter D'Onghia, both of whom managed to squeeze in a little proofreading between the odd birthday celebration or three (replete with slices of Hummingbird cake). Penelope Richardson came up with another of her classy masterpieces for the cover and Han Than Tun excelled with his wonderful illustrations. Richard Plunkett put clues to crosswords and Fabrice Rocher laid the whole thing out with patience and panache.

The original Lonely Planet Swahili phrasebook, from which the new edition developed, was written by Robert Leonard.

CONTENTS

INTRODUCTION

KARIBU!

Welcome! The word that greets you as a visitor to East Africa expresses the hospitality that will so often be extended throughout your stay. The word for 'stranger' in Swahili, mgeni, is also the word for 'guest' - and many East Africans enjoy the opportunity to welcome strangers as guests to their countries. We hope you will enjoy your time as mgeni. Communication in Swahili is the key to having a good time as you travel around East Africa, meet people, and feel the full extent of their welcome. This phrasebook will help you get started with Swahili and negotiate some of the situations you may experience along the way.

The Swahili language has a long and complicated history. It is a member of the Bantu language family found in Africa's mid-section. The Bantu langages have been spoken on the Indian Ocean coast from at least as early as the first millenium AD. Centuries of trade along the coast saw the influx of many linguistic influences from Arabic. By the time Portuguese ships began calling at East African ports in 1498, a version of the Swahili language was spoken by the coastal inhabitants, the WaSwahili, and over time a few Portuguese elements slipped into the language. While the Tanzanian mainland's three decades as a German colony had surprisingly little influence on Swahili, numerous words have been borrowed from the English (who colonised Kenya and then took control of what is now Tanzania). Generally, the Swahili people have kept the foreign words for the objects foreigners brought with them, such as kitabu from the Arabic *kitab* for 'book', mvinyo from the Portuguese *vino* for 'wine', and baisikeli for 'bicycle'. These imports behave grammatically as Swahili, but look and sound like their foreign ancestors.

Interaction with ocean-going trading ships probably provided the inspiration for the coastal Swahili people to travel inland in search of things to trade, including ivory. By 1800 long trade routes extended from the coast all the way across Lake Tanganyika. In the 19th century Arab and Swahili slave traders were combing the East African interior for slaves to work the plantations of Zanzibar and for export to Arabia. Traders, slavers, and later European explorers moved inland with large parties of Swahili porters from the coast. The language established itself as the medium of trade throughout much of the region, though people away from the coast continued to speak hundreds of other languages in their daily lives.

The importance of Swahili continued to grow throughout the 20th century. First, missionaries and colonial governments sought to simplify their tasks by encouraging Swahili as a standard language in Kenya and Tanzania. At the same time, citizens sought to master the language as they travelled to work on far-off plantations, engaged in trade, or went to schools. Later, the post-colonial independent governments in Tanzania and Kenya promoted Swahili as their national language. (English remains an official language of government in both countries, though Kenyans are generally more proficient in English than their Tanzanian neighbours.) Swahili as a lingua franca is spoken by many people in Uganda, Rwanda, Burundi, southern Somalia and northern coastal Mozambique. A version of Swahili is spoken as a first language by several million people in the eastern part of R. D. Congo (formerly Zaire). Most people in Kenya today speak at least some Swahili, and throughout Tanzania it is fast replacing local tongues as the first language of the new generations of children.

'Standard' Swahili is the language spoken in Zanzibar City. Several other variants, or dialects, of Swahili exist, notably those centered in Mombasa and Lamu. People inland often speak a somewhat less polished Swahili, or mix in elements from their own mother tongues. Congolese speakers have pronunciation differences and mix in a bit of French. Kenyans are especially prone to taking shortcuts with the language, and jokes abound about the roughness of Nairobi Swahili. Transcripts from our research, however, show that inland Tanzanians who have spent their entire lives in remote rural corners of the country speak a Swahili every bit as complex as that spoken on Zanzibar. Written Swahili, the language of newspapers, textbooks and literature, usually conforms to the coastal standards. In this book we tend toward standard coastal Swahili, but other elements may have seeped in from other parts of the Swahili-speaking world.

ABBREVIATIONS USED IN THIS BOOK

adj	adjective
lit	literally
n	noun
pl	plural
sg	singular
Tanz	Tanzania
v	verb

HOW TO USE THIS PHRASEBOOK
You *Can* Speak Another Language

It's true – anyone can speak another language. Don't worry if you haven't studied languages before, or that you studied a language at school for years and can't remember any of it. It doesn't even matter if you failed English grammar. After all, that's never affected your ability to speak it! And this is the key to picking up a language in another country. You don't need to sit down and memorise endless grammatical details and you don't need to memorise long lists of vocabulary. You just need to start speaking. Once you start, you'll be amazed how many prompts you'll get to help you build on those first words. You'll hear people speaking, pick up sounds from TV, catch a word or two that you think you know from the local radio, see something on a

INTRODUCTION

billboard – all these things help to build your understanding. In fact, this is just the way children learn to talk – certainly a proven method worldwide!

Plunge In!

There's just one thing you need to start speaking another language – courage. Your biggest hurdle is overcoming the fear of saying aloud what seem to you to be just a bunch of sounds. There are a number of ways to do this.

Firstly, think of some 'foreign' words or phrases you are familiar with. Such as *sayonara* and *hasta la vista* (both ways of saying goodbye), *que sera, sera* (remember that one!?). Well ... these are all 'foreign' languages you know, and people actually use them! In fact, if you say *sayonara* to a Japanese person, they'll probably reply with the same. You would have just had a conversation in Japanese! The point is: you are capable of saying a phrase fluently in another language - and you'll even get a response. From these basic beginnings, provided you can get past the 'courage to speak' barrier, you can start making sentences. Don't worry that you're not getting a whole sentence right the first time. People will understand you if you stick to the key words of the sentence. And you'll find that once you're in the country, it won't take long to remember the complete sentence.

The best way to start overcoming your fear is to memorise a few key words. These are the words you know you'll be saying again and again, like 'hello', 'thank you' and 'how much?'. Here's an important hint though: right from the beginning, learn at least one phrase that will be useful but not essential. Such as 'good morning' or 'good afternoon', 'see you later' or even a conversational piece like 'lovely day, isn't it?' or 'it's cold today' (people everywhere love to talk about the weather). Having this extra phrase (just start with one, if you like, and learn to say it really well) will enable you to move away from the basics, and when you get a reply and a smile, it'll also boost your confidence. You'll find that people you speak to will like it too, as they'll understand that at least you've tried to learn more of the language than just the usual essential words.

Key Words & Phrases to Memorise

Hello.	Salama.
Thank you.	Asante.
Please.	Tafadhali.
You're welcome.	Karibu sana.
(don't forget this one!)	
How much is it?	Kiasi gani?
Goodbye.	Tutaonana.
today	leo
tomorrow	kesho
Where is ...?	... iko wapi?
hotel	gesti; hoteli
restaurant	mkahawa; hoteli
bus station	stesheni ya basi
train station	stesheni ya treni

Ways to Remember

There are several ways to learn a language. Most people find they learn from a variety of these, although they usually have a preferred way to remember. Some like to see the written word and remember the sound from what they see. Some like to just hear it spoken in context. Others, especially the more mathematically inclined, like to analyse the grammar of a language, and piece together words according to the rules of grammar. The very visually inclined like to associate the written word and even sounds with some visual stimulus, such as from illustrations, TV and general things they see in the street. As you learn, you'll discover what works best for you – be aware of what made you really remember a particular word, and if it really stuck in your mind, keep using that method.

Kicking Off

Chances are you'll want to learn some of the language before you go. The first thing to do is to memorise those essential phrases and words. Check out the basics (page 45) ... and don't forget

INTRODUCTION

that extra phrase (see Plunge In!). Try the sections on making conversation or greeting people for a phrase you'd like to use. Write some of these words down on a separate piece of paper and stick them up around the place. On the fridge, by the bed, on your computer, as a bookmark for the book you're reading – somewhere where you'll see them often. Try putting some words in context – the 'How much is it?' note, for instance, could go in your wallet.

Building the Picture

We include a chapter on grammar in our books for two main reasons.

Firstly, some people have an aptitude for grammar and find understanding it a key tool to their learning. If you're such a person, then the grammar chapter in a phrasebook will help you build a picture of the language, as it works through all the basics, finishing with some examples of how you can create your own sentences.

The second reason for the grammar chapter is that it gives answers to questions you might raise as you hear or memorise some key phrases. You may find a particular word is always used when there is a question – check out the grammar heading on questions and it should explain why. This way you don't have to read the grammar chapter from start to finish, nor do you need to memorise a grammatical point. It will simply present itself to you in the course of your learning.

Any Questions?

Try to learn the main question words (see page 43). As you read through different situations, you'll see these words used in the example sentences, and this will help you remember them. So if you want to hire a bicycle, turn to the Hiring Vehicles section in Getting Around (use the Contents or Index pages to find it quickly). You've already tried to memorise the word for 'where' and you'll see the word for 'bicycle'. When you come across the sentence 'Where can I hire a bicycle?', you'll recognise the key words and this will help you remember the whole phrase. If there's no category for your need, try the dictionary (in our books, the question words are repeated there too, with examples).

Speaking in Tongues

Sorry but ... it's one of those things you just have to do. Especially if you're trying to remember the language before you go there. Do it while you're driving, out for a walk, washing the dishes. Talk to yourself, using all the new words you've learnt. If you like, imagine a scenario and act it out in your head. Say 'good evening' to an imaginary hotel owner (who doesn't, of course, understand English!), 'I'd like a room'. 'For the night'. 'For two nights'. 'I'd like a room for two nights ... please'. 'What a wonderful day it is today!' Well, why not? No-one can hear you – and what does it matter if they think you're crazy? Imagine what they'll think when, one day, they see you chatting happily with people in another language. Then the tables will be turned!

I've Got a Flat Tyre

Doesn't seem like the phrase you're going to need? Well, in fact it could be very useful. As are all the phrases in this book, provided you have the courage to mix and match them. We have given specific examples within each section. But the key words remain the same even when the situation changes. So while you may not be planning on any cycling during your trip, the first part of the phrase 'I've got ...' could refer to anything else, and there are plenty of words in the dictionary that, we hope, will fit your needs. So whether it's 'a ticket', 'a visa' or 'a condom', you'll be able to put the words together to convey your meaning.

INTRODUCTION

Finally

Don't be concerned if you feel you can't memorise words. On the inside front and back covers of our books are the most essential words and phrases you'll need. You could also try tagging a few pages for other key phrases, or use the notes pages to write your own reminders.

PRONUNCIATION

Perhaps the easiest part of learning Swahili is the pronunciation. While Swahili literature has ancient roots, it was only formalised as a written language during the 20th century. All the tricky sounds were written down by English speakers in standardised phonetic patterns, so once you learn a few basic rules you can pronounce pretty much anything you can read – well, you could pronounce anything if it weren't for the complicated twists and turns that the grammar makes you take. In this book we won't make you worry about words like tungalidang'anyi-shwa, which means 'were we to have been deceived'. Most words that you come across will roll off your tongue much more easily!

PRONOUNCE EVERY LETTER

Every letter gets pronounced, unless it is part of the consonant combinations discussed below. If a letter is written twice, it is pronounced twice – or rather, gets extended into two syllables. For example, mzee, which means 'respected elder', has three syllables: m-ZE-e. Note that the 'm' is a separate syllable, and that the practical effect of the double 'e' is to lengthen the vowel sound so that the word follows rule 2, with the stress on 'ze'.

STRESS

The stress almost always goes on the second-to-last syllable. There are a few dozen words out of the tens of thousands in Swahili that break this rule, so consider it a sign of your progress if you find yourself having to worry about any of them!

VOWELS

Vowels, the key to making your words understood, are as pronounced in Spanish or Italian. Readers of this book may have learned their English anywhere from Sydney to Kyoto to Belfast to Vancouver, so suggesting 'standard' English equivalents is difficult. If the following guidelines don't work for you, listen closely to how Swahili speakers pronounce their words and spend some time practising. (Alternatively, you can use the audio pronunciation guide on the World Wide Web to learn before you go, on: http://www.yale.edu/swahili/sound/pronounce.htm).

Remember that if two vowels appear next to each other, each must be pronounced in turn. For example, kawaida, 'usual', is pronounced ka-wa-EE-da.

PRONUNCIATION

a	as in 'calm' (dada, 'sister')
e	as the 'a' in 'may' (wewe, 'you')
i	as the 'e' in 'me' (sisi, 'we')
o	as in 'go' (moja, 'one')
u	as the 'o' in 'to' (duka, 'store')

CONSONANTS

r   Swahili speakers make only a slight distinction between r and l. The name Laurence, for example, might be written 'Raurence', 'Laulence', or even 'Raulence'! However, if you use a light 'd' where you read 'r', as in Spanish words 'para' or 'caro', you will usually be pretty close. The hard 'r' of many English speakers will often be understood, but only because East Africans are forgiving listeners.

dh   as 'th' in 'this' (dhambi, 'sin')

th   as 'th' in 'thing' (thelathini, 'thirty')

ny   as the 'ni' in 'onion' (nyasi, 'grass')

ng'   as in 'singer' (ng'ombe, 'cow'). A bit tricky at first - try saying 'sing' over and over again, eventually dropping the 'si', and this is how it sounds at the beginning of a word

gh   a guttural sound, similar to the ch in Scottish loch or as in the German ich (ghali, 'expensive')

g   as in 'get' (gari, 'car')

ch   as in 'church' (chakula, 'food')

GRAMMAR

Like all languages, Swahili is not simple. There are aspects of the grammar that may at first seem daunting, especially if you're already familiar with the grammar of an Asian or European language. Don't be disheartened though, because with a little time and practice things will start to make sense, and you'll soon find that putting simple sentences together is not really that hard.

SENTENCE STRUCTURE

The good thing about Swahili grammar is that even though there are many little rules to learn, these rules are very regular and have very few exceptions. The main task in starting out is learning how nouns and verbs work. Nouns behave differently depending on what class they fall into, and they in turn determine what prefixes verbs and adjectives will take.

Verbs are basically made up of a stem onto which a number of prefixes are added. These prefixes vary according to tense and to what class the noun they follow belongs to. There are also a few suffixes and infixes which can be added to verbs to create different meanings, but the majority of the information needed to create simple and effective Swahili sentences is carried by the prefixes.

Word Order

The basic word order in Swahili sentences is subject-verb-object, as in English – 'I (subject) read (verb) the book (object)'.

Grandma reads the book.   Bibi anasoma kitabu.
(lit: grandma she-*present*-reads book)

It is very important to understand the grammatical principle behind subject and verb because of the particular way the two interact in Swahili. Put simply the subject is the 'doer' of the verb-action. In the example above 'grandma' is the doer of the verb-action 'reading'.

NOUNS

Swahili divides its nouns into a number of noun classes that are usually distinguishable by various prefixes which have different singular and plural forms. Perhaps the most important thing to know about Swahili nouns is the particular effect they have when they act as the subject in a sentence. In those circumstances the class they belong to determines what the 'subject prefix' attached to the front of the verb will be. This means that there are a great number of possible combinations of prefixes that must be learnt in order to put nouns and verbs together to form sentences.

In this book we have devised a much simpler way to put sentences together that will help you get started. While not being grammatically correct in every detail our 'survival' Swahili will be totally comprehensible to the East Africans you encounter. As your familiarity with the language grows, you'll be able to put together some of the more complex noun-verb prefix combinations.

We therefore recommend you learn the singular and plural prefixes for all the major noun classes, but when constructing verbs and forming sentences, limit yourself to distinguishing nouns as either animate (people and animals), or inanimate (things) only. Don't worry too much about the proper form of the subject prefix for the verb because Swahili speakers will forgive poor grammar if your vocabulary is right.

You can already begin to see how influential the class of a noun can be in any given sentence. Put simply, you have one set of rules for how the classes act on nouns, and associated but dissimilar sets of rules for how they act on verbs, pronouns, adjectives and adverbs. Swahili learners often receive a big chart that lays out all the transformations on a grid, but it takes months to understand the chart and years to use it effectively. By starting with our 'survival' Swahili method, you can avoid the complications of the system and still make yourself understood.

Noun Prefixes

The first things to learn are the basic noun classes and their relative prefixes. The two most common are often called the m-wa class (for people and creatures only) and the n- class.

Singular		Plural	
m-		wa-	
mtoto	child	*watoto*	children
mlinzi	guard	*walinzi*	guards
(n)-		(n)-	
nyumba	house	*nyumba*	houses
baisikeli	bicycle	*baisikeli*	bicycles

You can see that some n- class nouns don't take any prefix, and all n- class nouns have the same form in both the singular and the plural. It's important to note, however, that when n- class nouns are the subject of a sentence the n- class subject prefixes attached to the verb will have different singular and plural forms.

Three other important noun class prefixes you will have to learn are:

Singular		Plural	
m-		mi-	
mti	tree	*miti*	trees
ki-		vi-	
kitabu	book	*vitabu*	books
(ji-)		ma-	
jicho	eye	*macho*	eyes
tunda	fruit	*matunda*	fruits

You should also be aware of the following noun classes:

Singular		Plural	
u-		–	
unwyele	hair	*nwyele*	hair(s)
u-		–	
uzuri	goodness		

GRAMMAR

Singular		Plural
ku- *kule* there		–
pa- *pale* there		–
mu- *mule* inside there		–

The subject prefixes which go with each noun class will be listed when we look at verbs and how to construct sentences.

Little Big Nouns

You can play with noun prefixes to indicate size. Using the ki/vi prefixes can indicate that something is a smaller version of the normal object. The ma prefix can be used to show that something is bigger than normal – but the catch is, since ma is a plural prefix, you have to plan sentences that reference more than one of whatever you want to augment.

	Singular	Plural

Normal	pikipiki
	    motorcycle
		pikipiki
		    motorcycles

Small	*ki*pikipiki
	    little motorcycle
		*vi*pikipiki
		    little motorcycles

Big	pikipiki kubwa* 	*ma*pikipiki big motorcycles

* 'big motorcycle' is pikipiki kubwa – kubwa, 'big', is the standard augmentative adjective which can be used almost universally

VERBS

The basic Swahili verb is simpler to master than that of most European languages; it's the more advanced permutations that can boggle the mind. Tenses are totally regular, so as long as you follow the rules correctly you won't need to memorise long lists of irregular verbs or complicated endings. By learning a few of the basic rules you'll be able to construct simple, serviceable Swahili verbs. We also mention some of the variations you may come across so that you're prepared if you hear them used, and can give them a try yourself.

Verb Stems & the Infinitive

You will often see verbs written in the infinitive form (such as in dictionary entries – English 'to be', for example). The infinitive in Swahili is formed by adding the prefix ku to a verb stem. In this book we show verbs without the ku, because it is always dropped when a verb is conjugated. The exception is verbs with one-syllable stems (such as kula, 'to eat'), which are always conjugated along with their ku infinitive prefix. It's still important to recognise both forms however, because in compound verbs you'll use the ku for the second (non-conjugated) verb.

Infinitive	Stem
kutaka (to want)	-taka
kufanya (to do)	-fanya
kusoma (to read)	-soma

What's in a Verb?

Information about the subject and the tense are tagged on to the verb stem in the following way:

	Subject Prefix	Tense Prefix	Verb Stem
ninasoma	ni	na	soma
I read	I	present	to read
alifanya	a	li	fanya
she did	she	past	to do

GRAMMAR

So – it's pretty easy to make basic verbs. All you need to do is take one subject prefix, add one tense prefix, and complete it with the verb stem. In the above examples the subjects of each sentence are animate and belong to the m-wa noun class. The verbs therefore takes m-wa class subject prefixes.

Notice how much activity happens within the verb! Also notice how important pronunciation is in making your meaning understood – every syllable in the verb is likely to have some grammatical meaning.

Subject Prefixes

To put together your own sentences, you'll need to know which subject prefix goes with which noun class. Using the 'survival' Swahili system you'll only have to learn the subject prefixes for the m-wa class (if the subject of the sentence is animate), and the n- class subject prefixes (for everything else).

If you feel confident enough to use the grammatically correct form of the subject prefix, you'll still find all the information you need in the following tables. Pronouns will be covered in their own section, but we introduce them here because you'll see them in this section.

Animate Subject Prefixes

	Noun Class Prefix	Subject Prefix	Pronoun	
singular	m-	ni-	mimi	I
	m-	u-	wewe	you
	m-	a-	yeye	he/she
plural	wa-	tu-	sisi	we
	wa-	m-	ninyi	you
	wa-	wa-	wao	they

Note that to express things in the negative, the m-wa class subject prefixes for first, second and third person singular (ni-, u- and a-) will change – negation is looked at on page 32.

Inanimate Subject Prefixes

	Noun Class Prefix	Subject Prefix	Pronoun	
sg	(n-)	i-	hii	it
pl	(n-)	zi-	hizi	they

The following examples show how the subject prefix at the start of each verb is determined by the noun class of the subject, in this case, 'who' or 'what' is doing the flying.

Sara flew the plane.   Sara ameirusha ndege.
                          (lit: Sara she-*recent*-it-fly-made plane)

Sara is flying the plane, therefore Sara is the subject of the sentence. As an animate she belongs to the m-wa class, the correct singular subject prefix is a-.

The plane flew Sara.   Ndege ilimruka Sara.
                          (lit: plane it-*past*-her-fly Sara)

The plane is flying Sara somewhere and is therefore the subject of the sentence. As a singular inanimate belonging to the n-class, the correct subject prefix is i-.

Here are the other subject prefixes. For 'survival' Swahili you'll only need to learn the correct noun class prefixes.

Noun Class Prefix		Subject Prefix	
singular	plural	singular	plural
m-	mi-	u-	i-
ki-	vi-	ki-	vi-
(ji-)	ma-	li-	ya-
u-	u-	zi-	–
u-	u-	–	–
ku-	–	ku-	–
pa-	–	pa-	–
mu-	–	mu-	–

GRAMMAR

Swahili nouns use the m-wa- class subject prefixes a- (sg) and wa- (pl) for almost all animate nouns regardless of how they shape their plural forms. For 'survival' Swahili, we suggest you use the n- class subject prefixes i- (sg) and zi- (pl) for all inanimate nouns. For example, even though the correct subject prefixes for the (ji)-ma- class are li- (sg) and ya- (pl) for all (ji)-ma- class inanimates, for animates you always use the m-wa- class subject prefixes a- (sg) and wa- (pl) – and in 'survival' Swahili you can use the n- class subject prefix i- (sg) and zi- (pl) for all inanimate (ji)-ma- class nouns. Just make sure you are careful to correctly differentiate between singular (i-) and plural (zi-) prefixes and you're ready to conjugate. The following examples show the 'survival' Swahili principle at work using the animate and inanimate (ji)-ma- class nouns jogoo, 'rooster'; majogoo, 'roosters' and jiwe, 'rock'; mawa, 'rocks':

GRAMMAR

		Correct Swahili	Survival Swahili
Animate		*singular* Jogoo anakaa ... The rooster sits ... *plural* Majogoo wanakaa ... The roosters sit ...	*singular* Jogoo anakaa ... *plural* Majogoo wanakaa ...
Inanimate		*singular* Jiwe linakaa mtoni. The rock sits in the river. *plural* Mawe yanakaa ... The rocks sit ...	*singular* Jiwe inakaa ... *plural* Mawe zinakaa ...

Tense Prefixes

To create the present, past and future, there are four tense prefixes that are placed within the verb.

na	present
li	past (completed actions)
me	past (recent or on-going actions)
ta	future

Present

The child wants a bike.　　Mtoto anataka baisikeli.
　　　　　　　　　　　　　(lit: child she-*present*-want bike)

Past (Completed)

The motorcycles went far.　Pikipiki zilienda mbali.
　　　　　　　　　　　　　(lit: motorcycles they-*past*-go far)

Past (Recent)

We have read the books.　　Tumesoma vitabu.
　　　　　　　　　　　　　(lit: we-*recent*-read books)

You've all done well.　　　Mmefanya vizuri.
　　　　　　　　　　　　　(lit: you-*recent*-do well)

Future

The guards will do work.　　Walinzi watafanya kazi.
　　　　　　　　　　　　　(lit: guards they-*future*-do work)

Will you want some fruit?　Utataka matunda?
　　　　　　　　　　　　　(lit: you-*future*-want fruit)

GRAMMAR

One-Syllable Verbs

Several verbs have stems that are only one syllable. In most tenses these verbs are conjugated along with their infinitive prefix ku. That is, when you construct sentences using one-syllable verbs, you retain the ku. The only tense where you'll need to strip the ku from these verbs is the present negative.

kula   to eat
    Ninakula chakula.   I am eating food.
     (lit: I-*present*-eat food)

kunywa   to drink
    Utakunywa maji?   Will you drink water?
     (lit: you-*future*-drink water)

kuja   to come
    Wazee wamekuja Gedi.   The elders have come to Gedi.
     (lit: elders they-*recent*-come Gedi)

kufa   to die
    Paka alikufa.   The cat died.
     (lit: cat he-*past*-die)

The verb kupa, 'to give', is an exception to the one-syllable exception – it behaves like a regular verb in dropping its ku, perhaps because in sentences it always takes an infix (to represent the person receiving), and therefore always has more than one syllable.

kupa   to give
    Unanipa kitabu.   You give me the book.

Other Tenses
Some verbs use markers other than the basic four.

- ki (if)
  Baba akikubali, mtaoana.
  If father agrees, you'll get married.
  (lit: father he-if-agree, you both-*fut*-marry)

- ki (when)
  I'll do it when I arrive.
  Nitafanya nikifika.
  (lit: I-*fut*-do I-when-arrive)

- nge (perhaps)
  If father agreed, you could marry.
  Baba angekubali, mngeoana.
  (lit: father he-perhaps-agree, you two-perhaps-marry)

- ka (same tense as previous verb – used in stories)
    Alikula, akajisaidia, akalala.
    He ate, then he went to the toilet, then he slept.
    (lit: he-*past*-eat, he-then-goes-to-toilet, he-then-sleep)

- mesha ('recent past'-'already')
    Nimeshamaliza.
    I have already finished.
    (lit: I-*recent*-already-finish)

- lisha ('past'-'already')
    Ilishaanguka.
    It already fell.
    (lit: it-*past*-already-fall)

Shortened Verb Forms

There is also a common variation on the present tense in which the na marker is contracted or left out. You can use this especially when talking about yourself – ni + na is contracted to na.

	Standard Form	Shortened Form
I want	ninataka	nataka
I read	ninasoma	nasoma
I come	ninakuja	nakuja

INFIXES

In the same way that prefixes are added to the front of a word, and suffixes to the end, infixes are added within words. In Swahili, object infixes are often inserted between tense prefixes and the verb stem. Throughout this book you will see instances where this occurs. The infix ji makes a verb reflexive – that is, it indicates doing something for oneself. You won't need to use infixes while you are in 'survival' Swahili mode, but we give a few examples so that you can be aware of them if they appear. A particularly important infix is po – it indicates 'when' or 'where'.

GRAMMAR

Verb without Infix	Verb with Infix
Tunategemea. We depend.	Tunajitegemea. We depend on *ourselves*.
Aliambia. He told.	Aliniambia. He told *me*.
Nitasaidia. I will help.	Nitajisaidia. I will use the toilet. (lit: 'I will help *myself*.')
Ninafika. I am arriving.	Ninapofika. *Where* I am arriving.
Utasoma kitabu. You will read the book.	Utakisoma kitabu. You will read (*it*) the book.

Sometimes more than one infix may appear in a single verb:

Unanipa.   Unaponipa.
You give it *to me*.   *When* you give it *to me*.

Except in the passive, the verb kupa, 'to give', always takes an infix – 'giving' is always done *to somebody*:

Nilimpa zawaidi.
I gave *her* a gift.

SUFFIXES
Swahili verbs can not only change at the beginning and the middle, but also at the end. Sometimes adding suffixes can change a-ending verbs to e-ending verbs. For survival purposes, there are five main suffixes to worry about – passive, causative, reciprocal, verbs that do 'to' or 'for' someone else, and ga.

Passive Suffix
Passive verbs reverse the action of the sentence, as in the English example, 'I read the book' (active), 'The book is read by me' (passive). In Swahili, passive verbs take the suffix wa.

Active	Passive
aliambia mimi he told me	aliambiwa mimi (lit: he-*past*-tell-*passive* by-me) he was told by me
anasoma kitabu she reads the book	kitabu kinasomwa naye (lit: book it-*present*-read-*passive* by-her) the book is read by her
alinipa she gave me	nilipewa naye (lit: I-*past*-give-*passive* by-her) I was given by her

Causative Suffix

A cool feature of Swahili verbs is that they can express being 'made to' or caused to do some action – and nouns can be turned into causative verbs. The usual suffix to show that something was made to happen is -sha, though many verbs take -za instead.

	Causative Form
Nitarudi. I will return.	Nitarudisha kalamu. I will give back (cause to return) the pen.
Anafika. She arrives.	Anafikisha barua. She delivers (causes to arrive) the letter.
umependa you liked	Umependeza. You are attractive (made likeable).
elimu education	Anaelimisha mtoto. He educates (causes to get an education) the child.

Reciprocal Suffix

The suffix -na expresses mutuality or doing for each other.

tunapenda we like	Tunapendana. We like each other.
walisaidia they helped	Walisaidiana. They helped each other.

'To' or 'For' Suffix

The suffixes -ia or -ea used with verbs often express the notion of 'to' or 'for':

Anaposta barua.	Ananipostia barua.
She mails a letter.	She mails a letter to me.
Ulipika chakula.	Ulipikia chakula kwa sisi.
You cooked food.	You cooked food for us.
Tutahama.	Tutahamia Arusha.
We will move.	We will move to Arusha.

'Ga' Suffix

The suffix -ga has no known function. Some say that it's not good Swahili, but you will hear it used all over East Africa. It seems that any verb can take ga at the speaker's whim. Because Swahili words are accented on the second-to-last syllable, adding the ga shifts the stress of the verb to what would otherwise be the final, unstressed syllable. This can be very confusing! Being aware that verbs can make such a shift may help you understand what Swahili speakers are saying.

For example, wanakula, 'they are eating', becomes wanakulaga, and alienda, 'she went', becomes aliendaga – note the change of stress within the words.

NEGATION

As you might expect, in Swahili the work of saying you 'don't' do something happens within the verb. To express things in the negative, you need to learn three new subject prefixes, one new rule for the present negative and two new past tense prefixes.

Negative Subject Prefixes	
si-	I do not
hu-	you (sg) do not
ha-	she/he does not
ha-	+ everything else does not

Note that the negative subject prefixes si-, 'I', hu-, 'you' and ha-, 'she/he', *replace* the standard ones listed on page 24 – these three prefixes denote 'people' (sg) only. In all other instances the negative subject prefix ha- simply goes in front of whatever standard subject prefix is being used. The full range of positive and negative 'survival' Swahili prefixes are:

	Animates		Inanimates	
	Pos.	Neg.		Pos.	Neg.
I	ni-	si-			
you (sg)	u-	hu-			
she/he	a-	ha-	it	i-	hai-
we	tu-	hatu-			
you (pl)	m-	ham-			
they	wa-	hawa-	they	zi-	hazi-

Negative Rule

The new rule for negatives governs some changes to the present, where you leave out the tense marker altogether. Verbs that end in -a become i-final, and one-syllable verbs usually drop their ku infinitive marker.

Here are some examples: (Note the sentences in which the subject is merely implied in the construction of the verb)

Subject	Subject Prefix(es)	Tense Prefix	Verb Stem	Negative Verb
I	si –	–	tak(a)i	sitaki
you (pl)	ha m	–	li	hamli
it	ha i	–	ruk(a)i	hairuki

Sitaki.	I don't want it.
Ninyi hamli nyama.	You all don't eat meat.
Ndege hairuki.	The aeroplane doesn't fly.

GRAMMAR

The following examples show the construction of present tense verbs in both affirmative and negative modes. As well as the use of a different subject prefix, you can clearly see how the tense marker is dropped and the a-final stems become i-final. Note that the bracketed present tense prefix na- is commonly omitted in the first person singular (see page 29); we include it here for the benefit of comparison with negative forms.

Affirmative		Negative	
Ni(na)jua.	I know.	Sijui.	I don't know.
Ni(na)elewa.	I understand.	Sielewi.	I don't understand.
Ni(na)weza.	I can.	Siwezi.	I can't.
Ni(na)kula nyama.	I eat meat.	Sili nyama.	I don't eat meat.
Unajua?	Do you know?	Hujui?	Don't you know?
Anaweza.	She/he can.	Hawezi.	She/he can't.
Tunapenda.	We like it.	Hatupendi.	We don't like it.

Negative Past Tense Prefixes

The two past tense prefixes have different forms in the negative. For a completed action in the past, the negative prefix ku- is used instead of the normal prefix li-.

Subject	Subject Prefix(es)	Tense Prefix	Verb Stem	Negative Verb
they	ha wa	ku	soma	hawakusoma
you (sg)	hu –	ku	la	hukula

| Watoto hawakusoma. | The children didn't study. |
| Hukula. | You didn't eat. |

For recent or on-going actions in the past, the normal prefix me- is replaced by the negative prefix ja-.

Subject	Subject Prefix(es)	Tense Prefix	Verb Stem	Negative Verb
I	si –	ja	kunywa	sijakunywa
we	ha tu	ja	fanya	hatujafanya

Sijakunywa maziwa.   I haven't drunk milk.
Hatujafanya bado.   We haven't done it yet.

Negative Future Prefix

The future marker ta is the same for both positive and negative.

Subject	Subject Prefix(es)	Tense Prefix	Verb Stem	Negative Verb
they	ha zi	ta	kuja	hazitakuja
she	ha –	ta	taka	hatataka

Pikipiki hazitakuja.   The motorcycles won't come.
Mama hatataka kazi.   Mother won't want work.

'TO BE'

Unlike many languages, the basic forms of kuwa, 'to be', are quite straightforward in Swahili. In most instances you can use a simple one-syllable word. 'To be something' is ni, the negative, 'not to be something' is si – you'll notice that these verbs correspond to the positive and negative subject prefixes for first person singular animates ('I' in the m-wa noun class). To express the past 'was' and the future 'will be', conjugate kuwa according to the rules for one-syllable verbs on page 27.

Yeye ni maskini.   He is poor.
Bob ni askari.   Bob is a soldier.
Si kitu.   It's nothing. (You're welcome.)
Si nzito.   It's not heavy.
Atakuwa daktari.   She will be a doctor.

GRAMMAR

To Be 'In' or 'At'

To express being 'in' or 'at a place' you use a subject prefix plus a locative prefix (ko, po, or mo). For 'survival' Swahili the only new subject prefix you'll need to learn is yu, 'she/he' – for all others you can use the standard ones (see pages 24 and 25). When choosing a locative prefix the differences between ko and po are too subtle to worry about. Use mo only to indicate something that is inside something else.

To make the sentence negative (*not* to be 'in' or 'at a place') you simply place the correct form of the negative subject prefix (si, hu, or ha) in front of the one you would use for an affirmative sentence.

Subject Prefix	Locative Prefix	
yu	ko	Yuko kanisani. She's at church.
hayu	ko	Hayuko kanisani. She's not at church.
i	ko	Nyumba iko Zanzibar. The house is in Zanibar.
hai	ko	Nyumba haiko Zanzibar. The house isn't in Zanzibar.
ni	po	Nipo pale. I'm there.
si	po	Sipo pale. I'm not there.

'TO HAVE'

'To have' in Swahili is expressed by the concept kuwa na, 'to be with'. In practice, you can express possession in the present tense by using the subject prefix (positive or negative) together with na. For other tenses, conjugate kuwa according to the rules for one-syllable verbs (see page 27), and add na.

Subject Marker	Tense Prefix	kuwa	na	
ni	–	–	na	Nina tikiti. I have a ticket.
a	–	–	na	Ana tikiti. She has a ticket.
hawa	–	–	na	Hawana tikiti. They don't have tickets.
si	–	–	na	Sina tikiti. I don't have a ticket.
a	li	kuwa	na	Ahmed alikuwa na tikiti. Ahmed had a ticket.

ADJECTIVES

Adjectives usually come after the noun they modify. For example:

nyumba kubwa (lit: house big)	a big house
nyumba ndogo (lit: house small)	a small house
mtu mkubwa (lit: person big)	a big person
mtu mdogo (lit: person small)	a small person

Some adjectives don't take prefixes, while others change prefix according to their noun. In this book we present the adjectives in the form correct for that context. We encourage you to practise making the adjectives agree with the nouns. Instead of listing the rules for each noun class, we suggest you make educated guesses based on the following patterns – there are many irregularities, as you'll see in the chart. If you see an adjective that begins with n, m, w, k, ch or v, it probably changes prefixes to agree with the class of the noun it modifies. If you use n or m as your prefix in such cases, you'll usually be OK.

rahisi	cheap
chumba/saa rahisi	cheap room/watch

GRAMMAR

GRAMMAR

ghali   expensive
  kiti ghali   expensive chair
  gazeti ghali   expensive newspaper

-swahili   Swahili
  mtoto mswahili   Swahili child
  viti vya kiswahili   Swahili chairs

-geni   foreign, strange
  watalii wageni   foreign tourists
  kitabu kigeni   foreign book

-eupe   white
  karatasi nyeupe   white paper
  mtu mweupe   white person

-eusi   black
  tai nyeusi   black tie
  watu weusi   black people

-ekundu   red
  chumba chekundu   red room
  nyumba nyekundu   red house

-zuri   good, nice
  habari nzuri   good news
  wasichana wazuri   good girls

-baya   bad
  habari mbaya   bad news
  wasichana wabaya   bad girls

-refu   tall, long
  twiga mrefu   tall giraffe
  shingo ndefu   long neck

-fupi   short
  miti mifupi   short trees
  meza fupi   short table

-ingi   many, much
  pesa nyingi   much money
  matunda mengi   many fruits

-chache	few
vyumba vichache	few rooms
mabasi machache	few buses
-zungu	European
Mzungu	white person
tabia ya kizungu	European habit
-kali	sharp, fierce
simba mkali	fierce lion
bia kali	sharp beer
-pole	gentle, kind
mvulana mpole	kind boy
upepo mpole	gentle wind
-tamu	sweet, delicious
chakula kitamu	delicious food
pipi tamu	sweet candy

PRONOUNS
Subject & Object Pronouns

Verbs are always marked with a subject prefix to show who or what is doing the action, so using subject pronouns isn't essential. However, they can be used to add greater clarity. In the following examples mimi, 'I', doesn't have to be used to make the meaning of the sentence clear, but it can add emphasis if it is used:

Ninataka watoto.	I want children.
Mimi ninataka watoto.	I (really) want children.
Nitapita posta.	I'll pass by the post office.
Mimi nitapita posta.	*I'll* pass by the post office.

A subject pronoun can never substitute for a subject prefix; if a construction requires a subject prefix, you must include it whether or not you use an independent pronoun. For example, Mimi tapita posta – for 'I'll pass by the post office' – is not a valid Swahili sentence.

GRAMMAR

Object pronouns are the same as their subject pronoun counterparts:

mimi	I, me	sisi	we, us
wewe	you (sg)	ninyi	you (pl)
yeye	she/he/her/him	wao	they/them

Demonstrative Pronouns

Instead of yeye, 'her/him' and wao, 'them', Swahili speakers often use the following demonstrative pronouns:

huyu	this person	hawa	these people
yule	that person	wale	those people

All-purpose demonstratives for things are:

hii	this (thing)	hizi	these (things)
hiyo	that (thing)	zile	those (things)

Yule bwana alikunywa bia hii.   That man drank this beer.

OBJECTS

Objects usually come after the verb:

Tunapenda nyama.	We like meat.
Hatuli nyama.	We don't eat meat.

Sometimes objects are placed before the verb to give emphasis:

Nyama tunapenda.	We like *meat*.
Nyama hatuli.	We don't eat *meat*.

POSSESSION

Swahili has seven stems to indicate possession, depending on who the object in question belongs to. These stems take different prefixes depending on the noun class of the object being possessed. Again the rules are complicated, and again you will usually be understood even if you use the wrong prefix. For 'survival' purposes, we suggest you use y as the prefix for all possessives. Other prefixes include z, w, ch, vy, l, mw, and kw.

GRAMMAR

Personal Pronouns

Possessive Stem	Recommended Pronoun	
-angu	yangu	my, mine
-ako	yako	your, yours (sg)
-ake	yake	his, her, hers, its
-etu	yetu	our, ours
-enu	yenu	your, yours (pl)
-ao	yao	their, theirs
-a Mary	ya Mary	Mary's
-a baba	ya baba	Father's

Possessive pronouns follow the object being discussed.

baisikeli yake	his bike
redio yetu	our radio
kemra yangu	my camera
saksi ya Fred	Fred's sock

PREPOSITIONS & CONJUNCTIONS

na   and, with

kuku na mayai	chicken and eggs
Nakaa na dada yangu.	I live with my sister.

kwa   to, by

Atakwenda kwa kaka yake.	He's going to his brother's place.
Tutakwenda kwa basi.	We'll travel by bus.

wa (sg), wa (pl)   of (for m-wa class, animates)

mtoto wa shangazi	the child of my aunt

ya (sg), za (pl)   of (for n- class)

mali ya taifa	wealth of the nation

lakini   but

Ningependa kwenda, lakini sina pesa.	I'd like to go, but I have no money.

GRAMMAR

au   or
> Unataka bia au soda?
> Do you want beer or soda?

kwamba   that
> Ameniambia kwamba ananipenda.
> She told me that she likes me.

ingawa   although
> Ancheza mpira wa kikapu ingawa ni mfupi.
> Although she's short she still plays basketball.

ila   except
> Nitakuazimu kila kitu ila gari langu.
> I'll lend you anything except my car.

kwa hivyo   therefore
> Nimechoka, kwa hivyo nakwenda kulala.
> I'm tired, therefore I'm going to bed.

kwa sababu   because
> Hutatoka nje kwa sababu kuna baridi.
> You won't go out because it's cold.

kama   like, if
> Anafanana kama baba yake.
> He looks like his father.
> Kama kuna mvua mazao yatastawi.
> If there's rain the crops will thrive.

angalau   even though
> Mtali alipiga picha ya simba angalua ilikuwa hatari.
> The tourist took a picture of the lion even though it was
>   dangerous.

yaani   that is
> Usinisumbue, yaani nipe amani!
> Don' bother me, that is, leave me alone!

GRAMMAR

ili   in order that
   Nipe pesa ili ninunue sukari.
   Give me money in order that I can buy sugar.

labda   perhaps
   Labda watarudi mwaka kesho.
   Perhaps they'll return next year.

QUESTIONS

There are two ways to form questions in Swahili. Neither involve changing the structure of your sentences. The easiest way
to indicate that you are asking a question is by beginning your
sentence with the word je. The best translation of je is 'Hey, I'm
asking a question'. Je can also be added to the verb as a suffix –
Ilikuwaje? 'How was it?'

You can also indicate that you are making an inquiry by
using a rising intonation at the end of your sentence. This
intonation is a little tricky – we recommend you practise with
a Swahili speaker.

Notice that there is no difference in word order between these
three sentences:

You can help me.	Unaweza kunisaidia.
Can you help me?	Unaweza kunisaidia?
	(spoken with a rising intonation)
Can you help me?	Je, unaweza kunisaidia?

Other than je, interrogative words usually go at the end of the
sentence.

Interrogative Words

nani   who
   Nani amekuandikia   Who wrote you that letter?
   barua hiyo?

gani   which/what/what kind
   Unasoma shule gani?   Which is your school?

GRAMMAR

nini   what
   Ulisema nini?
   What did you say?
   Hii ni nini?/Ni kitu gani?
   What is this?
   Unataka nini?
   What do you want?

kwa nini   why
   Kwa nini unasafiri peke yako?
   Why are you travelling alone?

lini   when
   Mgeni atarudi lini?
   When will the guest return?

vipi/namna gani   how
   Unasonga ugali namna gani?
   How do you make ugali?

wapi   where
   Soko liko wapi?
   Where is the market?

ngapi   how many
   Ni kilomita ngapi kwenda Nairobi?
   How many km's to Nairobi?
   Ni saa ngapi?
   What time is it?

(Note the placement of je within the conjugated verb 'to be'.)

GRAMMAR

MEETING PEOPLE

GREETINGS

You can never spend too long with greetings in East Africa. 'Hi, where's the bus', for example, is so brief that many people would find it rude. Greetings vary depending on whether you are speaking to one person or several, or to an older person. People will often spend several minutes with hands clasped, catching up on all the latest news. Pay attention to the many gestures that accompany greetings – respectful curtsies, grasped upper forearms, hand kisses or cool handshakes. Expect to shake hands with many people you meet. If your right hand is full or dirty, offer your wrist instead.

Respectful Greetings

When greeting an older person or an authority figure, start with:

Shikamoo.	Respectful greetings.

To which can be added:

mzee	respected elder
mama	mother (appropriate for any woman old enough to have children)
baba	father (appropriate for any man old enough to have children)

The usual reply is:

Marahaba.	Thank you for your respectful greetings.

Older people may sometimes greet younger foreigners with shikamoo , a carryover from colonial days when all white people demanded deference from Africans. An appropriate response is asante – 'thank you for your respectful greetings'.

Children often greet adult strangers by calling out shikamoo , and will be delighted if you reply with a warm marahaba . In many areas they'll run towards you with both hands raised above their heads. You can kneel or squat for them to place their hands on your forehead while they greet you, but if they've been outside playing you're within your rights to say:

Nawa, halafu nisalimie.   Wash your hands, then greet me.

After this respectful greeting you'll usually continue by exchanging one or many of the standard greetings below.

Jambo

Jambo is pidgin Swahili, used to greet tourists who are presumed not to understand the language. There are two possible responses, each with different connotations:

Jambo.   Hello, now please speak to me in English.

Sijambo.   Things are not bad with me, and I'm willing to try a little Swahili.

In some situations even long-term residents may choose to use jambo when they don't want to engage in conversation.

Jambo is the root of a verb that means 'to be unwell'. When used in common greetings, it's conjugated in the negative, 'to not be unwell'. This can be complicated, so memorise the following and think of it as 'to be fine'.

How are you? (to one person)	Hujambo?
I'm fine.	Sijambo.
How is (father)?	(Baba) hajambo?
(Father) is fine.	Hajambo.
How are all of you?	Hamjambo?
We're fine.	Hatujambo.
How are (your grandmother and grandfather)?	(Bibi na babu) hawajambo?
They are fine.	Hawajambo.

MEETING PEOPLE

Habari/Salama

Habari means news, and getting news is the main purpose of exchanging greetings. You can get news about pretty much anything, so the variations on this greeting are infinite.

Among the variations on 'habari' greetings, you may hear salama substituted for habari, or the habari may be dropped altogether. So if someone asks: Za leo?, reply as though they asked Habari za leo? – say Nzuri, Salama or Safi.

How are you?	Habari?
What's the news?	Habari gani?
Good morning.	Habari za asubuhi?
Good day.	Habari za leo?
Good afternoon.	Habari za mchana?
Good evening. (including night)	Habari za jioni?
What's up with you?	Habari yako?
How are you all?	Habari zenu?
How's everyone at home?	Habari za nyumbani?
How's work?	Habari za kazi?
How are you now?	Habari za saa hizi?
(if you've already seen each other that day)	

By memorising these three simple words, you can reply to almost anything:

Good.	Nzuri.
Fine.	Salama.
Clean.	Safi.

There are many more possibilities. Sometimes the replies may surprise you. Habari za nyumbani? 'How's everyone at home?', for instance, might be answered Hawajambo, 'Everyone's all right'.

If things are just OK, add tu after nzuri, salama, or safi. Even if things are really bad, most people will reply to greetings with nzuri tu rather than mbaya, 'bad'.

If things are really good, you can add sana, 'very', or kabisa, 'totally', after nzuri, salama, or safi.

Salama is perhaps the most useful word in the Swahili language. You can always use it to greet anybody you pass on the street, or to reply to any greeting said to you.

'COOL' GREETINGS

Younger people have dozens of cool ways to greet each other, including special handshakes. Although no book can give you up-to-the-minute slang, the phrases in this section seem likely to stay cool into the 21st century.

Mambo?	How's things?
Sasa?	Now?
Vipi?	What's up?
Sema.	Say.
Lete habari.	Bring news.
Je?	What?

Possible replies include:

Fresh.	Fresh.
Poa.	Cool.
Safi.	Nice.
Fiti.	Fit.
Kazi.	Work.

Hodi & Karibu

When you want to enter someone's home or office, you should always call out hodi before crossing the threshold. Hodi announces your presence and your intent to come in, and can be accompanied by knocking on the door. Even if you're being escorted in by the inhabitant, it's polite to pause at the doorway and say hodi.

You will always be greeted with karibu – 'welcome'. Karibu is an all-purpose word, used to welcome visitors to the home, the business, or even the country. It also means: 'You're welcome'.

Welcome to my home.	Karibu nyumbani.
Welcome inside.	Karibu mpaka ndani.
Have a seat.	Karibu kukaa/kiti.
Welcome to Zanzibar.	Karibu Zanzibar.
Bon appétit!	Karibu chakula!
(lit: welcome to food)	
Welcome again.	Karibu tena.
You're quite welcome.	Karibu sana.

FIRST ENCOUNTERS

East Africans are usually happy to talk with new people. After a few greetings, you may want to ask each other your names. People will probably pronounce your name somewhat differently than you are used to. After a while, you can start introducing yourself by your 'new' Swahili name.

What's your name?	Jina lako nani?
	Unaitwa nani?
	Unaitwaje?
My name is ...	Jina langu ni ...
	Naitwa ...
How are the children/ parents/relatives?	Watoto/Wazazi/ Jamaa hawajambo?
What have you come here for?	Kwa nini umekuja hapa?
For a holiday.	Kwenye livu.
For tourism.	Kutalii.
Where are you going?	Unakwenda wapi?
I'm going to ...	Nakwenda ...
We're going to ...	Tunakwenda ...

YES, NO, THANK YOU

Swahili has several ways to say yes, and there's no hard and fast rule for the use of each:

Yes.	Ndiyo/Mmmm.
Yeah.	Nnh.
OK.	Sawa/Haya.

There are also a few ways to say no:

No.	Hapana.
Not even.	Hata.
It's not so.	Sivyo.
Uh-uh.	Uh-uh/Mm-mm.

There are also several ways to say thank you:

Thank you. (to one person)	Asante/Aksante/ Ahsante.
Thank you very much.	Asante sana.
Thank you. (to more than one person)	Asanteni (sana).
I thank you. (to one person)	Nashukuru.
Thanks to you.	Shukrani.

On the other hand, saying 'no thank you' can be difficult. Say asante with a hand motion to signal 'stop', and perhaps the sound 'uh-uh'.

How long have you been here?	Umekaa siku ngapi hapa?
I've been here for three weeks.	Nimekaa hapa wiki tatu.
We've been here four days.	Tumekaa hapa siku nne.
When did you arrive?	Ulifika lini?
What day did you come?	Ulikuja siku gani?

Please. (when asking for a real favour)	Tafadhali.
Excuse me.	Samahani.
Maybe.	Labda/Pengine.
OK.	Sawa.
Is there a problem?	(Vipi) kuna shida?
No problem.	Hakuna shida.
It's nothing.	Si kitu.
Don't worry about it.	Usie na wasiwasi.
Just joking!	Natania tu!
	Ni utani!
Take it easy.	Usiwe na wasiwasi.
May I take a picture?	Naomba kupiga picha.

It's polite for others to ask the news of the place you've just come
from. This often generates a long and friendly conversation in
which people ask you about your family, job, recent news they've
heard on the radio, etc.

Where are you coming from?	Unatokea wapi?
Where have you just been?	
I'm coming from ...	Natokea ...
home	nyumbani
the fields	shambani
a safari	safarini
the market	sokoni
the forest	porini/mwitumi
town	mjini
drawing water	kuteka/kuchota maji
the cinema (the movies)	sinema
school	shuleni/shule/skuli
university	chuo kikuu
How are things in ...?	Habari ya/za ...?
town	mjini
England	Uingereza
Fine.	Nzuri.

MEETING PEOPLE

Goodbyes

In contrast to the amount of time people spend greeting each other, East Africans put relatively little energy into saying goodbye. Often farewells simply involve confirming when you'll next meet, then walking away with a simple haya. Saying goodbyes before a long trip is more involved; hands clasped, the traveller is wished well and told to greet everybody at their destination.

OK.	Haya.
Tomorrow.	Kesho.
Later on.	Baadaye.
Good night.	Usiku mwema.
We'll see each other.	Tutaonana.
Farewell.	Kwa heri.
Have a good trip.	Safari njema.
Greet everyone for me.	Wasalimie.
Regards to your mother.	Msalimia mama.

BODY LANGUAGE & ETIQUETTE

Even though in material terms conditions for many are harsh, people are generous in friendship – once you develop your photographs of East Africans, you'll notice how many smiles you took away with you! Naturally, people who travel in touristed areas will sometimes be preyed upon by the unscrupulous – so take adequate precautions, and then relax. Your hosts will appreciate a guest whose manner shows enjoyment.

Due to cultural differences, your body language may convey many subtle but wholly unintentional messages. For example, if you stand deferentially with your hands in your pockets, people may interpret you as standing 'like the boss' – instead, clasping your hands behind your back or crossed over your chest will render you unobtrusive. On the other hand, nobody will think you the slightest bit rude if you casually pick your nose. Men can even stand in a public place urinating, as long as they face away from people; women should squat discretely behind a tree or clump of grass.

Men and women maintain a formal distance in many social situations. Women usually show physical deference when greeting people of either gender, including curtsies and hand kisses. Public displays of affection between the sexes do not happen! In many parts of East Africa women will feel intensely uncomfortable if alone with a man who is not a blood relative or husband. Women also do not make flamboyant displays of their bodies – although breastfeeding a baby is always acceptable. On the other hand, friends of the same sex often hold hands while walking around town. Feel honoured if someone of your gender makes such a display of friendship. Close female friends may even stroke each other in ways that could be wrongly interpreted as sexual.

It's fine to wear shorts in tourist areas, but you'll give the impression of being childish. East African youths spend hours ironing their clothes with hot coals in cast irons – neatness is valued and will get you far. Long pants or skirts are essential when visiting government offices or people's homes, and are preferable at most other times.

People eat and shake hands with their right hand, and 'wipe' with their left. If someone would like to greet you by shaking hands and you're eating, offer your wrist instead. Pointing at someone says 'beware'. Beckoning with your index finger and your palm upraised is obscene. Showing the bottom of your feet, such as putting them up on a stool or coffee table, is openly rude.

MEETING PEOPLE

Hitchhiking, kuomba lifti, is common, though you may be expected to pay for a ride. The universal raised thumb couldn't stop a tortoise in East Africa. Instead, a wave of the arm will signal most drivers that you're looking for a ride. Local buses will stop if you simply extend your arm fully and flap your hand like a whale's tail. If a vehicle stops for you, the common greetings don't apply – drivers are always in a hurry. Instead, say: Bwana, unaweza kunisaidia kwenda …? 'Mr, can you help me get to …?'

Attracting Someone's Attention

To attract the attention of someone from a distance, a loud sudden hiss can stop them in their tracks. The beckoning gesture is with arm extended, palm downwards.

Come here.	Njoo.
You!	Wewe!
Stop!	Simama!
Wait!	Subiri!

Mwizi! is the cry to stop a thief. However, calling mwizi may cause a mob scene in which the suspect is badly beaten or even killed. Also, in major cities the men who give chase just might be in cahoots with the thief. It's much better not to travel with anything you aren't prepared to lose, especially on public transport and in the cities.

LANGUAGE DIFFICULTIES

Many people in East Africa understand simple English. Even if you're shy of your Swahili, you can try to initiate conversation in English, but it is always better to dare and learn by mistakes. Keep your head – at worst you can expect several minutes of confusion.

Do you speak English/Swahili?	Unasema Kiingereza/ Kiswahili?
I don't speak English/Swahili.	Sisemi Kiingereza/Kiswahili.

Does anyone here speak English?	(Je,) kuna mtu ambaye anasema Kiingereza hapa?
A little.	Kidogo.
Do you understand?	Unaelewa?
I understand.	Naelewa.
I don't understand.	Sielewi.
Please speak slowly.	Tafadhali sema pole pole.
Please say that again.	Tafadhali sema tena.
Do you have a translator?	(Je,) kuna mtafsiri hapa?
How do you say ... in Swahili?	Unasemaje ... kwa Kiswahili?
Can you read this for me?	Unaweza kunisomea hiki?
Please write ... for me in English.	Tafadhali niandikie ... kwa Kiingereza.
Wait, I'll try to find it in this book.	Subiri kidogo nitajaribu kuitafuta katika kitabu hiki.

NATIONALITIES

Unfortunately we can't list all countries here, however you'll find that many country names are similar to English.

Where are you from?	Unatoka wapi?
	Kwenu ni wapi?
	(lit: 'Where is your place?')
I'm from ...	Natokea ...
	Kwetu ni ...
	(lit: 'Our place is ...?')
Africa	Afrika
Asia	Eshia
Australia	Australia
Canada	Kanada
China	Uchina
Djibouti	Jibuti
Egypt	Misri/Ijipti
England	Uingereza

MEETING PEOPLE

Eritrea	Eritrea
Ethiopia	Etiopia/Uhabeshi
Europe	Ulaya
France	Ufaransa
Germany	Ujerumani
Greece	Ugriki
India	Uhindi/Indiya
Ireland	Ayalendi
Israel	Uyahudi/Israeli
Italy	Italia
Japan	Ujapani
the Middle East	Mashariki ya kati
Russia	Urusi
South America	Amerika ya kusini
the USA	Marekani/Amerika
West Africa	Afrika ya magharibi

What part of America/England? — Marekani/Uingereza sehemu gani?

What's your your place of birth/residence? — Unatoka wapi?

What's your nationality? — Wewe ni mwenyeji wa wapi?
I'm a citizen of the USA. — Mimi ni mwenyeji wa Marekani.

I'm from America. — Natoka Marekani.

LANGUAGES

To form a language name in Swahili, add the prefix ki to the name of the people:

Arabic	Kiarabu
Chinese	Kichina
English	Kiingereza
French	Kifaransa
German	Kijerumani

MEETING PEOPLE

Italian	Kitaliani
Japanese	Kijapani
Russian	Kirusi
Somali	Kisomali
Spanish	Kihispania
Swahili	Kiswahili

AGE

How old are you?	Una umri gani?
	Una miaka mingapi?
	(lit: 'How many years do you have?')
I'm (26).	Nina miaka (ishirini na sita).

(See Numbers & Amounts, page 149 to learn how to say your age.)

OCCUPATIONS

| What work do you do? | Unafanya kazi gani? |

I'm a/an ...	Mimi ni ...
artist	msanii
business person	mfanyabiashara
secretary	karani
accountant	mhasibu
cook	mpishi
dentist	mganga wa meno
diplomat	mfanyakazi wa ubalozi
doctor	daktari/mganga
driver	dereva
engineer	fundi
farmer	mkulima
guide	kiongozi
journalist	mwandishi wa habari; ripota
lawyer	mwanasheria
merchant/trader	mwuzaji/mfanyabiashara
musician	mwanamuziki
nurse	mwuguzi

MEETING PEOPLE

photographer	mpigapicha
politician	mwanasiasa
scientist	mwanasayansi
soldier	askari/mwanajeshi
tailor	fundicherahani
teacher	mwalimu
tradesperson	mfanyabiashara
translator	mtafsiri/mkalimani
traveller	msafiri
unemployed	mtu asiye na kazi
	(lit: a person who doesn't have a job)
waiter	mfanyakazi/mtumishi

I'm unemployed.	Mimi sina kazi.
I study at (Machakos school).	Nasoma (shule ya Machakos).
I'm here for work.	Ninakaa hapa kwa ajili ya kazi.

STUDYING

I study at (Machakos) school.	Nasoma shule ya (Machakos).
I'm here for school.	Ninakaa hapa kwa ajili ya shule.

classroom	darasa
school fees	ada za shule
school uniform	nguo za shule
primary school	shule ya msingi
secondary school	sekondari
student/students	mwanafunzi/wanafunzi

RELIGION

Travellers are often asked about religion. The majority of East Africans adhere to Islamic or Christian faiths. Most Christian denominations are established in one or another region. Conversely, Judaism and the Eastern religions are almost unheard of.

MEETING PEOPLE

What is your religion?	Dini lako ni nini?
I'm …	Mimi ni …
Buddhist	Mbudisti
Catholic	Romani/Mkatoliki
Christian	Mkristu
Orthodox	Muortodoks
Hindu	Mhindu
Jewish	Myahudi
Muslim	Mwislamu
Protestant	Mprotestanti
Lutheran	Mluteri
I'm not religious.	Sina dini.

FAMILY

Are you married? (addressing a woman)	Umeshaolewa?
Are you married? (addressing a man)	Umeshaoa?
I'm married. (woman speaking)	Nimeolewa.
I have a husband.	Nina mume.
I'm not married yet.	Sijaolewa bado.
I'm married. (man speaking)	Nimeoa.
I have a wife.	Nina mke.
I'm not married yet.	Sijaoa bado.
Is your wife here?	Mke wako yuko huko?
Who are you with?	Uko na nani?
I'm with …	Niko na …
Do you have children?	Una watoto?
How many … do you have?	Una … wangapi?

MEETING PEOPLE

I have (two) ...	Nina ... (wawili)
children	watoto
brothers and sisters	kaka na dada
I have neither brothers nor sisters.	Mimi sina kaka wala dada.
I don't have many relatives.	Mini sina jamaa wengi.

Extended Family

Swahili kinship connections through your father's brothers and your mother's sisters are regarded very highly. Rather than being 'uncles' and 'aunts', they're considered your parents. If they are older than your birth parents they are 'big' (mkubwa), if they are younger they are 'little' (mdogo). All the children from your father's brothers are your brothers and sisters.

family	familia
mother	mama
father	baba
sister (older/younger)	dada (mkubwa/mdogo)
brother	kaka
younger brother	bwana mdogo
my older brother	mkubwa wangu
sister/brother-in-law	shemeji
aunt (mother's older sister)	mama mkubwa
aunt (mother's younger sister)	mama mdogo
aunt (father's sister)	shangazi
uncle (mother's brother)	mjomba
uncle (father's older brother)	baba mkubwa
uncle (father's younger brother)	baba mdogo
grandmother	bibi
grandfather	babu
wife	mke
husband	mume
child/children	mtoto/watoto

daughter
  binti

son
  mvulana

fiancé/e
  mchumba

girl/boyfriend
  mpenzi

HEY BROTHER

The word ndugu means 'brother' in the broad sense, and can be used to mean comrade, close friend or close kin - and it works for either a man or a woman.

OPINIONS

Conversing and debating with friends is an important part of daily life in East Africa. People express strong opinions about sport, politics and the latest local gossip. Diplomatic restraint is the visitor's best approach when talking about things that may be locally controversial – but if you have strong opinions about problems in your own country, speak your mind without worry.

What do you want?	Unataka nini?
I want ...	Nataka ...
I don't want ...	Sitaki ...
Do you like ...?	Unapenda ...?
I like ...	Napenda ...
I don't like ...	Sipendi ...
What do you think about ...?	Unafikiri nini kuhusu ...
I agree.	Nakubali.
I don't agree.	Sikubali.
I'm right.	Nina haki.
You're right.	Una haki.
Really?	Kweli?
Really!	Kweli!
It's surprising.	Inashangaza.
	Ni ajabu.
That's true.	Ni kweli.
That's not true.	Si kweli.

MEETING PEOPLE

I think/believe ...	Nadhani .../Naamini kwamba
...	
I think so.	Nadhani hivyo.
I don't think so.	Sidhani.
Right? (is it so?)	Sivyo?
Listen!	(Ebu) sikiliza!

FEELINGS

Swahili speakers express feelings with the verb 'to have' rather than 'to be', as we do in English. Many of these feelings can also be expressed with nasikia, 'I feel', but the simple form below will always be understood.

I'm ...	Nina ...
I feel ...	Nasikia ...
angry	hasira/kasirika
cold	baridi
depressed	sikitiko/sikitika
happy	furaha/furahi
hot	joto
hungry	njaa
right	haki
sad	sikitiko/sikitika
thirsty	kiu
tired	uchovu/uchofu

I'm happy!	Nafurahi!
I'm angry.	Nakasirika.
I'm sad.	Nasikitika.
Great!/Brilliant!/Fantastic!	Safi!/Barabara!
	(pronounced ba-RA-ba-ra)
Beautiful!	Maridadi!
I like Kenya very much.	Ninapenda Kenya sana.

INTERESTS

| I like/I don't like to ... | Napenda/Sipendi ... |
| dance | kucheza densi |

go to the movies	kuona filamu
play cards	kucheza kadi
play sports	kufanya michezo
read	kusoma
sing	kuimba
go to the theatre	michezo ya kuigiza
travel	kusafiri
watch TV	kutazama televisheni
write letters	kuandika barua

What do you do after work?	Unafanya nini baada ya kazi?
Let's dance.	Tucheze tafadhali.
	(Ebu) njo tucheze.

ARRANGING TO MEET

Where are you staying?	Unakaa wapi?
I'm staying at …	Nakaa …
Please give me your address/ phone number.	Tafadhali nipe anwani/ simu yako.
What's the address?	Ni anwani gani?
Can we meet again?	Tunaweza kuonana tena?
When will we meet again?	Tutaonana lini tena?
Let's meet (at three o'clock).*	Tuonane (saa tisa).
Let's go for a coffee.	Twende kunywa kahawa.

*See page 139 for information on the Swahili system of telling the time.

STAYING IN TOUCH

What's your address?	Anwani yako ni nini?
I'll send you a letter.	Nitakutumia barua.
I'll write to you.	Nitakuandikia (barua).
I'll telephone you.	Nitakupigia simu.
I'll visit you.	Nitakutembelea.

MEETING PEOPLE

MEETING PEOPLE – CROSSWORD

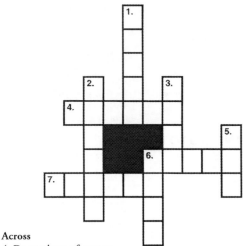

Across
4. Descendants of parents
6. A single female offspring
7. Current events, important recent happenings

Down
1. Get hip by greeting people with this
2. Word said to someone you're glad to receive or allow in
3. Greeting used when entering someone's home
5. State of hydration after a long day in the sun
6. Another term for a mother's mother-in-law

Answers on page 223.

GETTING AROUND

One of the most common ways of getting around in East Africa is by bus or on small minibuses called daladala (Tanz) or matatu (Kenya). Daladala and matatu are usually used for shorter trips to and from towns. They are often overcrowded and not particularly comfortable, but because they are readily available and inexpensive, they are one of the best ways to move about and sample the local life. In cities, daladala/matatu and taxis are the best means of transportation.

Trains are fine for longer trips and provide an excellent opportunity to admire the countryside, but they tend to be very slow and are not always reliable.

Flying is another alternative for travel between large cities (Dar es Salaam to Arusha, for example). There's a good network of internal flights within Kenya but much less so in Tanzania, Uganda, Rwanda, Burundi and Zaire. Flights to smaller towns and cities generally have to be arranged with smaller, private airlines and tend to be very expensive.

FINDING YOUR WAY

Remember to always exchange greetings before asking any of these questions.

Excuse me, I'm looking for …	Tafadhali, natafuta …
Excuse me, can you help me?	Tafadhali, naomba msaada.
I want to go to …	Nataka kwenda …
I'm looking for …	Natafuta …
Is it far?	Ni mbali?
Is it close to here?	Ni karibu?
How many kilometres from here?	Ni kilomita ngapi kutoka hapa?
Where's the (bus stop)?	(Bas stendi) ni wapi?

GETTING AROUND

Which ... is this?	Hii ni ... gani?
street	mtaa
highway/road	barabara
city	mji
province/region	mkoa
village	kijiji
address	anwani

DIRECTIONS

There are a few things to be aware of when asking for directions in Swahili. Since highways are not marked for distance with kilometre or mile posts, most East Africans have their own ideas about how far a kilometre really is. Most people walk long distances on a daily basis and their concept of distance may be very different from yours. For example, if you ask where the market is, you may be told it's 'just over the hill' or more likely, 'over there'. The person giving directions may fail to mention that 'over there' is a two-hour hike.

Turn/Go ...	Kata/Pita/Chukua ...
left	kushoto
right	kulia
straight ahead	moja kwa moja

Turn around.	Kata/Geuka.
Turn back.	Rudi nyuma.

above	juu ya
below	chini ya
there	huko
over there	pale
next to	jirani/karibu na
map	ramani

east	mashariki
west	magharibi
north	kaskazini
south	kusini

THEY MAY SAY ...

Meli/basi/ndege imechelewa.

The boat/bus/plane is delayed.

north-east	kaskazini masbariki
north-west	kaskazini magbaribi
south-east	kusini masbariki
south-west	kusini magbaribi

BUYING A TICKET

| What time is the … leaving? | … inaondoka saa ngapi? |
| Is the … leaving today/ tomorrow? | … inaondoka leo/kesho? |

aeroplane	ndege
bus	basi
truck	lori
motorcycle	pikipiki
minibus	daladala (Tanz); matatu (Kenya); basi
train	treni; gari la moshi

| What time will we leave/ arrive? | Tutaondoka/Tutafika saa ngapi? |

Are there seats available?	Kuna nafasi?
I'd like to buy a ticket.	Nataka kununua tikiti.
I'd like to buy two tickets.	Nataka kununua tikiti mbili.

Can we stop over in …?	Tunaweza kupitia …?
How much per person?	Ni bei gani kwa kila mtu?
How much for the ticket?	Tikiti ni bei gani?
I'd like to make a reservation to go to …	Nataka kufanya buking kwenda …
I'd like to change my ticket.	Nataka kubadilisha tikiti yangu.
I'd like to refund my ticket.	Tafadhali, unirudishie nauli yangu.
I'm sorry, I've changed my mind.	Samahani, nimebadili nia.

GETTING AROUND

Is this seat available?	Je, naweza kukaa hapa?
This seat's taken.	Kuna mtu anayekaa hapa.
Excuse me. (I'm sorry)	Samahani.
Can I put my bag here?	Naweza kuweka mzigo wangu hapa?

AIR

aeroplane	ndege
aeroplane tickets	tikiti ya ndege
airline	kampuni ya ndege
airport	uwanja wa ndege; kiwanja cha ndege
departures	wanaoondoka
arrivals	wanaofika
flights	wanaosafiri
What time is the plane leaving?	Ndege itaondoka saa ngapi?

BUS

As mentioned earlier, there are a variety of different buses in East Africa. Travelling by bus is definitely the cheapest form of transportation, but it can also be one of the slowest since they make frequent stops. It's best to buy tickets for long trips the day before you want to travel in order to get a seat on the bus – it's not unusual for a bus to be packed to the aisles.

Buses rarely run on schedule since they often won't leave until they're full. Be prepared to be approached by employees of the bus companies whose sole purpose is to get you on their bus. They will tell you anything to achieve this goal, so beware. If you ask if the bus is leaving now, you will be reassured that the bus is leaving right at that moment even if it's not due to depart for another two hours. There are many bus companies and some have better reputations than others. It's better to ask around before travelling. Make sure you keep your bags with you at all times.

bus	basi
bus station	stesheni ya basi
bus stop	bas stendi; kituo cha basi
minibus	daladala (Tanz)/matatu (Kenya)/basi

Is there a bus going to …?	Kuna basi ya …?
Which bus goes to …?	Basi gani inakwenda …?
What time is the bus leaving?	Basi inaondoka saa ngapi?
What time does the first/last bus leave?	Basi ya kwanza/mwisho inaondoka saa ngapi?
Where does this bus leave from?	Basi inaondoka kutoka wapi?
Where do I/we get on the bus?	Nipande/Tupande basi wapi?

Please tell me when the bus arrives in (Arusha).	Basi ikifika (Arusha), tafadhali unijulishe.
I want to get off here.	Nitashuka hapa.
Drop me off!	Shusha!
Stop!	Simama!

TRAIN

Trains travel very slowly, making frequent stops along the way. If you're not in a hurry, the train can be a very relaxing way to travel and see the countryside. It's also a safer way to travel than the bus, but the trains often break down. Therefore, it's best not to depend on them if you have to get to your destination on time.

SHUSHA!

Shusha! is the most common word people call out to get a bus to stop. It's also considered slang. If you pay attention to the way East Africans deliver the line, then casually call shusha the same way when you want to get off, you can sometimes bring an entire bus to laughter.

GETTING AROUND

You can usually travel in 1st, 2nd or 3rd class. If a man and a woman wish to share a compartment, they usually have to travel 1st class. Men and women are usually separated in 2nd class compartments, but they're usually comfortable. You'll find that 3rd class is essentially standing room only.

train	treni; gari la moshi
train station	stesheni ya treni
1st class	daraja la kwanza
2nd class	daraja la pili
3rd class	daraja la tatu

What time does the train leave/ arrive?	Treni itaondoka/itafika saa ngapi?

BOAT

There are a number of different kinds of boats available for transport along the coast. Large boats and ferries (meli) are used to cover long distances, while a number of smaller vessels are used for shorter journeys. The dhau, or traditional Swahili sailing boat, is popular among tourists to travel short distances to nearby islands, although it's highly recommended you only ride in a boat with a motor in case the winds fail. Smaller boats with outboard motors, mashua, are often used for short distances and to carry passengers from larger boats to the shore.

meli	ship
dhau	traditional sailing boat
mashua	small wooden boat with an outboard motor
mtumbwi	row boat

Where do we get on the boat?	Tupande meli wapi?
What time does the boat leave/arrive?	Meli inaondoka/inafika saa ngapi?
Where's the restroom?	Choo kiko wapi?

| I feel sick. | Najisikia mgonjwa. |
| I'm going to vomit. | Nataka kutapika. |

We're going (daily).	Tunakwenda (kila siku).
We're late.	Tumechelewa.
We want to arrive early.	Tunataka kufika mapema.

coast	pwani	passenger(s)	abiria
early	mapema	seat	kiti
fast	haraka	slow	pole pole
harbour/dock	bandari	space/room	nafasi
mainland	bara		

TAXI

In East Africa, taxis can take a variety of shapes and forms. The majority have no signs on them indicating that they are a taxi. Many are dilapidated old cars with missing door handles, windows and doors that don't work, etc. Taxi drivers usually stand near their cars soliciting passengers. You should always agree on a price before you get in as the taxi driver is likely to give you an outrageous price. It's best to ask an unbiased third party what a fair price is beforehand. Taxis can be scarce at times, particularly in smaller towns so it's also not unusual to share a taxi with strangers. Each person usually agrees on their fare individually, depending on how far they're going.

| taxi | teksi |
| taxi stand | stendi ya teksi |

| Where are you going? | Unakwenda wapi? |
| What's the fare? | Nauli ni bei gani? |

How much to go to …?	Ni shilingi ngapi kwenda …?
That's too expensive.	Ni ghali mno.
Can you lower the price (more)?	Tafadhali punguza bei (zaidi)?
Agreed. Let's go.	Sawa. Twende.

GETTING AROUND

I want to go to ...	Nataka kwenda ...
Please drive slowly.	Tafadhali, endesha pole pole.
Stop here.	Simama hapa.
We've arrived.	Tumefika.
Can you wait for me?	Tafadhali, uningojee?
Can you wait here?	Unaweza kungoja hapa?
I/we don't want a taxi.	Sitaki/Hatutaki teksi.

HIRING VEHICLES

Usually bicycles and motorcycles can be hired in areas where there are a lot of tourists, such as near the coast or in Zanzibar. Cars are difficult to hire. Sometimes legally established businesses require you to sign an insurance form. There are also plenty of enterprising individuals willing to hire out their own bicycles or motorcycles for short periods of time. If you get a flat tyre, there are a surprising number of places to get it fixed, since so many people own bicycles themselves.

I'd like to hire a ...	Nataka kukodi ...
car	gari
motorcycle	pikipiki
bicycle	baisikeli

GETTING AROUND

How much?	Ngapi?
What's the price …?	Ni bei gani kwa …?
per day	siku
per week	wiki
per month	mwezi
for (three) days	siku (tatu)

Can you lower the price?	Tafadhali, punguza bei.
How much is insurance?	Bima ni bei gani?
I/we don't want a car.	Sitaki/Hatutaki gari.

engine	injini
insurance	bima
mechanic	fundi
motor oil	mafuta ya gari
petrol (gasoline)	petroli
petrol station	stesheni ya petroli
tyre	tairi
rim (tyre)	rimu
wheel	gurudumu

(For useful phrases on hitchhiking, see page 54.)

Breakdowns

I've got a flat tyre.	Nilipata pancha.
The tyre blew out.	Tairi ilipasuka.
The (car) broke down.	(Gari) limeharibika.
The battery died.	Betri ilikufa.
Can you repair it?	Unaweza kuitengeneza?

GETTING AROUND

GETTING AROUND – CROSSWORD

Across
1. Baby street
3. May one enquire as to the price?
5. Quicker than medium pace
7. Financial protection from misfortune
8. Home to villagers

Down
1. The fastest way to travel between continents
2. 13 Skid Row 90210, for example
4. Two-wheeled flying chair
6. Mombasa and Nairobi are two examples

Answers on page 223.

ACCOMMODATION

FINDING ACCOMMODATION

East Africa has a wide variety of accommodation on offer which varies greatly in price and comfort. There are a number of luxury hotels and resorts which cater for the many tourists who come for safaris or to visit the coast, but moderate to very cheap accommodation is also readily available. Along the coast and on Zanzibar, there are also a number of 18th and 19th century Swahili, Arab and Indian houses that have been made into beautiful guesthouses and are quite reasonably priced. Single, double and triple rooms are often available, even in smaller hotels. A 'suite' usually means that a small sitting room is available in addition to sleeping quarters and a bathroom.

guesthouse	gesti
hotel (also restaurant)	hoteli

Excuse me, is there a hotel nearby?	Samahani, kuna hoteli hapa karibuni?
Is this a hotel/guesthouse?	Hii ni hoteli/gesti?
Is there a place to stay here?	Kuna mahali pa kukaa hapa?
We need a place to stay.	Tunahitaji mahali pa kukaa.
Can I/(we) stay here?	Je, (tu)naweza kukaa hapa?

CHECKING IN

Do you have a room?	Je, kuna nafasi ya chumba hapa?

Is there (a) ...?	Je, kuna ...?
air conditioning	AC
bath	bafu
electricity	umeme
fan	feni
key	ufunguo

ACCOMMODATION

hot water	maji ya moto
toilet	choo
telephone	simu

THEY MAY SAY ...

Watu wangapi?	How many persons?
mtu mmoja	one person
watu wawili	two people

How much per ...?	Ni bei gani kwa ...?
night	usiku
week	wiki
month	mwezi

I'll stay for two/three nights.   Nitakaa kwa usiku mbili/tatu.

That's too expensive.   Ni ghali mno.
Can you lower the price?   Naomba upunguze bei.

Can I look at the room?   Nataka kuangalia chumba?
Do you have any other rooms?   Kuna vyumba vingine?
What's my room number?   Chumba changu ni namba
    gani?

I want a/an ... room.	Ninataka chumba ...
ordinary	cha kawaida
cheaper	cha bei rahisi
larger	kikubwa zaidi
smaller	kidogo zaidi
quieter	ambacho hakuna kelele

bed	kitanda
bedroom	chumba cha kulala

breakfast	chai cha asubuhi
entrance	mahali pa kuingilia
exit	mahali pa kutokea
food	chakula
lift (elevator)	lifti
lights	taa
room	chumba
rooms	vyumba
vacant/occupied	kuna/hakuna nafasi

ACCOMMODATION

REQUESTS & COMPLAINTS

I/we need (a) ...	Ninahitaji/Tunahitaji ...
another bed	kitanda kingine
blanket	blanketi
firewood	kuni
glass	glesi
mosquito coils	dawa ya mbu
mosquito net	chandalua
pillow case	foronya/mfuko wa mto
pillow	mto
sheet/sheets	shuka/mashuka
soap	sabuni
toilet paper	karatasi ya choo
towel	tauli

I can't lock/unlock the door.	Siwezi kufunga/kufungua mlango.

DID YOU KNOW ...

A fully grown hippopotamus can weigh as much as 2600kg and though they may look sluggish they're capable of running very fast!

ACCOMMODATION

Can you clean the room?	Tafadhali, safisha chumba.
This room isn't clean.	Chumba hiki hakina usafi.
There's no hot water.	Hakuna maji ya moto.
Can you repair it?	Unaweza kuitengeneza?
Is there electricity?	Je, kuna umeme?
Did the electricity fail?	Umeme umekatika?
The … doesn't work.	… haifanyi kazi.
The … broke.	… imeharibika.

CHECKING OUT

We'd like to check out.	Tunataka kuondoka.
We'd like to pay now.	Tunataka kulipa sasa.

bill
   risiti
receipt
   risiti
tax
   kodi

LEAVE IT OUT!

Sometimes the present tense marker na can be contracted or left out. You can do this especially when talking about yourself, eg 'I want' nataka/ninataka.

Can I store my bags here?	Je, naweza kuacha mizigo yangu hapa?
Put it here.	Weka hapa.
I/we will return in two weeks.	Nitarudi/Tutarudi baada ya wiki mbili.

LAUNDRY

Most hotels offer laundry services. Even in rural areas, there is usually a dobi (washer woman/man) who will wash and iron clothes for a fee. The dobi will wash all articles of clothing except, sometimes, underwear.

washer woman/man	dobi	to iron	kupiga pasi
iron (n)	pasi	to wash clothes	kufua nguo

FEELING DIRTY?

When having your clothes washed, starching will be an option available even to budget travellers.

Ask for:

Usiweke stachi.	Without starch.
Weka stachi.	With starch.

Can you wash these clothes?	Tafadhali, unifulie nguo hizi.
Where can I wash these clothes myself?	Je, kuna mahali pa kujifulia nguo mwenyewe?
Is there a laundry service near here?	Kuna dobi hapa?
These clothes are not very clean.	Nguo hizi siyo safi.
Please wash them again.	Tafadhali, fua nguo tena.

ACCOMMODATION

ACCOMMODATION – CROSSWORD

ACCOMMODATION

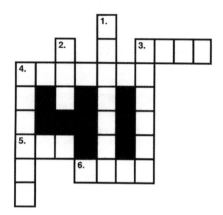

Across

3. Device for transmitting speech
4. Human fuel
5. Supports your head at night
6. They'll get even the worst stains out

Down

1. Easily misplaced opening device
2. Illuminating electrics
3. Good to wash with, bad to eat
4. Typically cuboid habitation space

Answers page 223.

AROUND TOWN

From the Swahili ruins on the coast to the spectacular game parks of the savannah, travelling in East Africa is a diverse and enriching experience. Both the cities and the villages offer a wide range of sights, services and social activities. Banking and services such as telecommunication centres are generally available only in cities and some large towns. Specialised services (such as shipping and international express services) tend to be concentrated in the capital cities. While many people speak excellent English in the cities, you'll need to know a few Swahili phrases for travel in the more rural areas or for just getting around town.

LOOKING FOR ...

Where's the ...?   ... ni wapi?
I'm looking for the ...   Natafuta ...
   bank   benki
   barber shop   kinyozi
   Catholic church   kanisa la RC
   cemetery   makaburi
   Christian church   kanisa la kikristo
   cinema   sinema
   ... embassy   ubalozi wa ...
   market   soko
   mosque   msikiti
   (national) museum   makumbusho (ya taifa)
   national monuments   kumbukumbu za taifa
   national park   mbuga ya taifa
   park (gardens)   bustani
   police station   kituo cha polisi
   post office   posta
   restaurant   mkahawa/hoteli
   ruins   maghofu
   school   shule
   tourist office   ofisi ya watalii

Is it nearby?	Ni karibu?
Is it far?	Ni mbali?
Is (the post office) open?	(Posta) imefunguliwa?
(The church) is closed.	(Kanisa) imefungwa.

For more useful phrases to help you find your way around see the Directions section on page 66.

AT THE BANK

The basic unit of Kenyan, Tanzanian and Ugandan currency is the shilling. There are a number of banks and exchange bureaus in all the major cities and even the smaller towns. Credit card services are limited to big cities and, even then, they're not generally accepted outside a few of the luxury resorts and safari lodges. Be aware that in Tanzania, credit cards cannot be used to obtain cash. You'll find that most banks have staff who speak English. In most places, service is very slow, so you may want to take that into account when planning your daily excursions. It's a good idea to hold on to your currency exchange receipts for the duration of your stay.

Where can I change some money?	Naweza kubadilisha pesa wapi?
Do you change money?	Unachenji?
I want to change money.	Nataka kubadilisha pesa.
What's the exchange rate?	Ni reti gani?
	Unabadilisha kwa ngapi?
How many shillings for one (dollar)?	Shilingi ngapi kwa (dola) moja?
I'd like to have money transferred from ...	Nataka kupokea pesa kutoka ...
How long will it take?	Itakuwa muda gani?
I'm expecting a money transfer from ...	Nasubiri pesa zilizotumwa kutoka ...

cheque	hundi ya benki
coins	chenji/fedha
currency	hela/pesa
foreign exchange bureau	benki/foreks
transaction receipt	risiti/stakabadhi

AT THE POST OFFICE

Post offices, posta, are located in all major towns. Service can be very slow and there's often no visible line or queue. Simply step up and try to hold your ground until you reach the window. Letters, postcards, aerograms, faxes and packages of almost any size can be sent out or received, but be prepared for problems with the customs department if you receive a package. In such an event, you will be expected to open it up in the presence of the customs officer who will look over the contents and assess the tax you are expected to pay, which can often be high. If you need to send a letter or package by express mail, there are international courier offices in the capital cities and some other larger centres. There are no facilities for registered and express mail within the local East African postal systems.

I'd like to send (a) ... to (Kenya).	Nataka kutuma ... (Kenya).
gift	zawadi
letter	barua
package	kifurushi, mzigo
luggage	mizigo
trunk (tea-chest)	sanduku

by airmail	kwa ndege
by sea	kwa meli

Is it permitted to send this?	Je, inaruhusiwa kutuma hii kwenye barua?
How much is it to send a (letter) to ...?	Ni shilingi ngapi kutuma (barua) kwenda ...?

Where can I post this?	Posta iko wapi?
(Three) stamps please.	Nataka stempu (tatu).
Is there any mail for me?	Je, barua zangu zimefika?
My name is …	Jina langu ni …
address	anwani
envelope	bahasha
mailbox (P.O. Box)	sanduku la posta (S.L.P.)
stamp	stempu

STREETLIFE

(Please) come here!	Njoo!
(Please) go away!	Hebu! Toka!
I don't have any money!	Sina hela/pesa!

The People

beggar	mwombaji/maskini
hawkers	wauzaji
hoodlum/riffraff	mhuni/wahuni (pl)
newspaper vendor	mwuzaji wa magazeti
street children	watoto wa mitaani
street hawkers	wauzaji barabarani
thief/thieves	mwizi/wezi
women food vendors	wanawake wanaouza chakula njiani

The Places

building/buildings	jumba/majumba
footpath	njia ya miguu
main street/highway	barabara kubwa
street	njia
traffic lights	taa za trafiki

AROUND TOWN

TELECOMMUNICATIONS

The best place to make long-distance phone calls is at 'telecom centres' – places similar to the post office where phone calls can be made and faxes sent or received.

Public telephones are now in many of the main cities and you can get phone cards at specific locations (information is usually written on the telephone booth).

Many city dwellers have taken to using cellular phones since the regular phone lines tend to be unreliable, particularly during the rainy season. In rural areas, calls can often be placed at the post office.

Making a Call

telephone centre	mahali pa kupiga simu
I'd like to make a phone call.	Nataka kupiga simu.
Where's the phone?	Simu iko wapi?
Is there a phone near here?	Je, kuna simu karibu na hapa?
I want to call …	Nataka kupiga simu …
The number is …	Ni namba …
How much is it per minute?	Ni shilingi ngapi kwa dakika moja?
Do you have a telephone directory?	Una kitabu chenye namba za simu?
I'd like to speak to an operator?	Nataka kuongea na opereta.

AROUND TOWN

SIGNS	
NI MARUFUKU/ HAIRUHUSIWI …	IT'S FORBIDDEN TO …
KUPIGA PICHA	TAKE A PICTURE
KUVUTA SIGARA	SMOKE
KUTUPA TAKATAKA	THROW RUBBISH
HAPA	HERE

SIGHTSEEING

No matter where you are, there are always plenty of opportunities to experience the diverse cultures of East Africa. Whether you're in the city or passing through a small village, the beauty of both the landscape and the people is astounding. East Africans are generally very hospitable and friendly, but try to respect local customs and privacy.

AROUND TOWN

    Always ask before taking anyone's picture. In areas where there are a lot of tourists, many of the residents have come to resent having their picture taken. Many will ask for a fee. Many Muslim women especially do not wish to have their photos taken, even when they are veiled. Curious glances into people's houses are not welcome and should be avoided if at all possible, particularly in crowded cities and towns such as Zanzibar.

    Always ask people if you are permitted to enter a building, particularly government buildings and mosques. Women are generally not permitted to enter mosques. There are certain restrictions on photographing government buildings and even bridges, so be careful what you photograph. On the other hand, people off the beaten track may request you take their picture and send them a copy – usually a fair trade if you keep your end of the bargain.

Am I allowed to take photographs here?	Je, inaruhusiwa kupiga picha hapa?
May I take your photograph?	Naomba kupiga picha yako.
Can you take my photograph?	Tafadhali, unipige picha.
I'll send you the photo.	Nitakupostia/Nitakutumia picha.
Give me your address so I can send the picture.	Nipe anwani yako ili nikutumie picha.
Can I look at …?	Je, naweza kuangalia …?
Can I touch it/hold it?	Je, naweza kugusa/ kushika hii?

PHOTOGRAPHING PEOPLE

The dark skin tones of many East Africans present a special challenge to photographers. Film processors often underexpose the darker elements of photographs so as to avoid overexposing the lighter parts of the picture, which in practice can ruin photos of African people. In order to be sure that the details of dark-toned faces are distinguishable in your processed pictures, we suggest a few tricks.

- Use your flash when taking pictures of Africans from closer than 4 or 5 metres, even in bright sunlight (and make sure you travel with extra batteries for your flash).

- Avoid photos where Africans are posed against bright backgrounds, such as when the sun is behind them.

- If people are wearing bright clothing such as white shirts, try taking the picture from the neck up – and again be sure to use the flash.

AROUND TOWN

AROUND TOWN

Excuse me, what is this/that?	Hii/hiyo ni nini?
What's the name of this/that?	Hii/hiyo inaitwa nini?
When was it made?	Ilitengenezwa mwaka gani?
Do you have a map?	Una ramani?
Is there a guide/translator available?	Je, kuna kiongozi/mtafsiri?
How much is it to get in?	Ada ya kuingia ni ngapi?
I want (three) tickets.	Nataka tikiti (tatu).

art gallery	duka la sanaa
artwork	sanaa
beach	baharini/ufukwe
bridge	daraja
building	jengo
cathedral	kanisa kuu
church	kanisa
game park	hifadhi ya wanyama
harbour	bandari
house	nyumba
jewellery store	duka la dhahabu
map	ramani
mosque	msikiti
national museum	makumbusho ya taifa
old stone town (of East African Coast)	mji mkongwe
river	mto
ruins	maghofu
university	chuo kikuu

DID YOU KNOW ... Many isolated roads in East Africa may be in a bad state of repair, so breakdowns and getting stuck – especially in the wet season – are regular features of any journey.

SIGNS

UWE MWANGALIFU	CAUTION
HATARI	DANGER
IMEFUNGWA	CLOSED
IMEFUNGULIWA	OPEN
MAHALI PA KUINGIA	ENTRANCE
MAHALI PA KUTOKA	EXIT
HAIRUHUSIWI KUINGIA	NO ENTRY
HAIRUHUSIWI KUPAK GARI HAPA	NO PARKING
USIVUTE SIGARA	NO SMOKING
MAELEZO	INFORMATION
MAPOKEZI	RECEPTION
SIMAMA	STOP
CHOO; MSALANI (WANAWAKE/WANAUME)	TOILETS (WOMEN/MEN)

ENTERTAINMENT

East Africa offers a variety of modern and traditional forms of entertainment. Urban areas offer a variety of restaurants, clubs and casinos, as well as more traditional forms of entertainment. In the villages, nightlife revolves around the local bar/restaurant. These places tend to be frequented more by men than women.

What's there to do around here?	Kuna starehe gani huku?
I want to go to a/an ...	Nataka kwenda ...
Where can I find a good ...	... nzuri iko wapi?
coffee house	mkahawa
bar	baa
cinema	sinema
nightclub	disco/baa
restaurant	mahali pa kula

AROUND TOWN

What film is showing?	Filamu ipi inacheza?
Is there a play showing?	Kuna mchezo?
How much is it to get in?	Kiingilio ni shilingi ngapi?
I want (three) tickets.	Nataka tikiti (tatu).

Let's go for ...	Twende ...
a coffee	kunywa kahawa
a dance	kwenye densi
dinner	kula
a drink	kunywa vinywaji

My treat!	Mimi nitalipa.

Traditional Dance & Music

In the villages, dances might be performed at certain ceremonies, such as harvest festivals, initiation ceremonies, and at weddings. These days, traditional dances can often be seen in town halls or on commons (open public areas) in more urban areas.

There are often national competitions for traditional dance, as well as dance troupes that make scheduled appearances. Local advertisements on street corners and word of mouth are the best sources for finding out about local events.

I want to see traditional dance with drumming.	Nataka kwenda kuona mchezo wa ngoma.
Great performance!	Mchezo safi (mzuri)!

band	kundi la wanamuziki; bendi/wapigamuziki
dance	densi
dancers	wachezaji wa densi
performance	mchezo
traditional dance	ngoma
traditional drumming/drums	ngoma

BUREAUCRACY

I'd like to …
  extend my visa
  visit the game park

Nataka …
  kupata visa nyingine
  kutembelea hifadhi ya
    wanyama

PAPERWORK

ada ya kuondoka	departure tax
anwani	address
bila ada	duty free
jina	name
kastam/forodha	customs
kazi/ajiria	occupation
maana ya kusafiri	purpose of stay
mpaka/hadi	valid until
muda wa kukaa	duration of stay
mwezi/tarehe/	month/date/
mwaka wa kuzaliwa	year of birth
namba ya pasipoti	passport number
nchi ya kuzaliwa	country of birth
nchi ya uraia	nationality;
	domicile (country of
	residence)
pasipoti	passport
tarehe ya kufika	date of arrival
tarehe ya kuondoka	date of departure
tarehe	date
tarehe/mahali pa kutolea	date/place of issue
ubalozi	embassy
uhamiaji	immigration

Do I require ...?	Je, ninahitaji ...?
I have (a/an) ...	Nina ...
entry permit	pemit ya kuingia
customs form	fomu ya forodha
driver's license	laiseni ya kuendesha gari
health certificate	cheti cha afya/daktari
identification	kitambulisho
papers	karatasi
pass/permit	cheti/cheti cha
passport	pasipoti
police report	ripoti ya polisi
receipt	risiti
visa	visa

I was robbed.	Niliibiwa.

See also the Emergencies chapter, page 153 for useful phrases when dealing with the police

See also the Emergencies chapter, page 153 for useful phrases when dealing with the police

AROUND TOWN

SHOPPING

East Africa has an amazing array of traditional goods to offer. Each region usually specialises in some art form, be it basket weaving or wood carving. Each urban area usually has one or many open marketplaces, as well as shops and curio stores filled with goods from all the regions. Although a few upmarket shops and boutiques may have fixed prices, the majority do not; bargaining is therefore essential. Most shops are open every day, including Sunday in some places. Many shops close at lunch time for approximately two hours, especially in the Muslim areas along the coast. In these areas, all Muslim-owned businesses close on Friday, and all activity comes to a standstill.

SHOPS

Is there a store near here?	Je, kuna duka hapa jirani?
Where can I buy ...?	Naweza kununua ... wapi?
I'd like to buy this/that.	Nataka kununua hii/hiyo.
Is there a store near here?	Je, kuna duka hapa jirani?

Where is a/an ...?	... ni wapi?
bakery	duka la mkate
barber	kinyozi
bookshop	duka la vitabu
butcher	duka la nyama
camera shop	duka la kemra
chemist/drugstore	duka la dawa
clothes shop	duka la nguo
fruit/vegetable shop	duka la matunda/mboga
general store/shop	duka/kioski
hairdresser (for braid or plaiting)	mahali pa kusukwa nywele
hairdresser (for cutting)	mahali pa kukata nywele/kinyozi

jewellery shop (for gold/stones)	duka la dhahabu
market	soko
music shop	duka la muziki/kanda
seamstress/tailor	mshonaji/fundi cherahani
shoe shop	duka la viatu
silver shop	duka la fedha
woodcarver's market	soko la makonde

MAKING A PURCHASE

How much is it?	Bei gani?
(Please) show me.	Naomba kuona.
	Nionyeshe.
I'm just looking.	Naangalia/Natazama tu.
Do you have others?	Je, kuna nyingine?
I want one/two.	Nataka moja/mbili.
I want a larger ...	Nataka ... kubwa zaidi.
I want a smaller ...	Nataka ... ndogo zaidi.
I want (one) like this.	Nataka (moja) kama hii.
I like this one/that one.	Napenda hii/hiyo.
I don't like it.	Sipendi.

THEY MAY SAY ...

Unataka ngapi?	How much/many do you want?
Hamna/Hakuna.	We don't have any available.
Haiwezekani.	It's not possible.
(Kredit kadi/hundi) ni nini?	What's a (credit card/cheque)?

| I want this/that. | Nataka hii/hiyo. |
| I don't want it. | Sitaki. |

What's this made of?	Ilitengenezwa kwa nini?
I'd like a refund.	Unirudishe/Nirudishe pesa.
Can I pay by (credit card/ cheque)?	Je, naweza kulipa na (kredit kadi/hundi)?

bag/backpack	mfuko
battery	betri
bottle	chupa
change	chenji
needle (sewing)	sindano
plastic	plastiki
plastic bag	begi (ya plastiki)
receipt	risiti
thread (sewing)	nyuzi

BARGAINING

How much is it?	Bei gani?
That's very expensive.	Ghali sana.
Is there a cheaper one?	Kuna nyingine ambayo siyo ghali?
Can you lower the price?	Tafadhali, upunguze bei.

I'll pay … shillings.	Nitalipa shilingi …
I can't pay more than … shillings.	Siwezi kulipa zaidi ya shilingi …
It's a fair price.	Ni bei nzuri/nafuu.
It's not a fair price.	Siyo bei nzuri.
Is that your final price?	Ni bei ya mwisho?
OK, I'll take it.	Haya, nakubali.

bottom price	bei ya mwisho
cheap	rahisi
(too) expensive	ghali (mno)

SHOPPING

SOUVENIRS

basket	kikapu/vikapu (pl)
bowls	bakuli
candlestick holders	mishumaa
colourful paintings	tingatinga (Tanz)
comb	kitana
copper tray	sinia ya shaba
folding safari chairs	kiti/viti
four legged stool/chair	kiti/viti
knife	kisu/visu
large ceramic pot	chungu
large, round, shallow basket (used for cleaning grains)	ungo
music cassette	kanda la muziki
plaited mat (traditional)	mkeka
shield	ngao
spear	mkuki
three legged stool	kigoda/vigoda
wood carvings	makonde
wooden spoon	kijiko/vijiko (pl)
Zanzibar chests/trunks	sanduku

TRADITIONAL DRESS & BODY DECORATIONS

Kanga
> traditional printed cloth bearing a proverb, worn in
> pairs by women. One kanga is usually worn over a
> dress or skirt to protect the clothing, the second may
> either cover the head or be used as a sling to carry a
> baby on the back.

Kikoi
> a solid coloured cloth with a decorative border. It's worn
> only by men, either on its own or under the kanzu.

Kanzu
> long cotton dress worn primarily by Muslim men. A kikoi
> is usually worn underneath it.

Kofia
> small hat worn by men

Buibui
> long covering worn by Muslim women to veil
> themselves. Traditionally the buibui is black, and one
> continuous piece is worn from the head down to the
> toes, leaving only the eyes showing. Today they are
> often different colours and usually have buttons or
> zippers.

Mtandio
> scarf worn to cover the head

Hina
> henna or natural red dye used to decorate the soles of
> the feet and the palms of the hands

Wanja
> Indian ink used to create intricate patterns on the hands
> and tops of feet

SHOPPING

CLOTH

Textiles in East Africa have different names, depending on their design, cultural meaning or purpose. Kanga and kitenge are often found in the market places. Kikoi are generally found along the coastal regions where they are worn by Muslim men either alone or under a kanzu.

kanga/kanga (pl)	cloth printed with proverbs (sold in pairs) for women
kikoi/vikoi (pl)	solid coloured cloth with decorative border (for men)
kitenge/vitenge (pl)	colourful cloths with printed design (for women)
kitambaa/vitambaa (pl)	regular cloth

CLOTHING

Can I try this (clothing) on?	Je, naweza kujaribu kuvaa (nguo) hii?
It fits well.	Inanienea/Inafaa vizuri.
It suits me very well.	Inanikaa kabisa.
Do you have something in my size?	Una nguo za saizi yangu? Una nguo za kunienea?
I want a larger ...	Nataka ... kubwa zaidi.
I want a smaller ...	Nataka ... ndogo zaidi.
It's too short.	Ni fupi mno.
It's too long.	Ni ndefu mno.
Can you shorten this?	Unaweza kufupisha hii?
Can you change the width?	Unaweza kubadilisha upana?
Can it be altered?	Unaweza kubadilisha hii?
Can you mend this?	Unaweza kushona hii?
When will it be ready?	Itakuwa tayari lini?

blouse	blausi	jumper/sweater	sweta
bra	sidiria/ sidilia	pants	suruali
		shirt	shati

clothes	nguo	shorts	kaptura
coat	koti	socks	soksi
dress	gauni	undershirt	fulana
hat	kofia	underwear	chupi
jacket	koti		

JEWELLERY & ACCESSORIES

bracelet	bangili
earrings	hereni;
	skurubu ya masikio
gloves	glovsi;
	soksi za mikono
jewellery	vipuli
necklace	mkufu
ring	pete
shoes	viatu
sunglasses	miwani ya jua
umbrella	mwavuli

TOILETRIES

If you're looking for an item not on this list, try using the English word for it. Most little kiosks will have soap, razors, toothbrushes and toothpaste, as well as the body oil that many East African women use to make their skin glow. Deodorant is not widely available. Women will sometimes have problems purchasing menstrual products; even if they are available, male clerks may hesitate to handle them. If you don't bring your special toiletries from home, you can often find them in the major towns, but at very high prices. Suntan lotion is generally unavailable outside the tourist hotels.

brush	burashi
comb	kitana/kichanuo
condom	kondom
insect repellent	dawa ya kuzuia mbuu
mirror	kioo
razor	wembe

sanitary napkins	Kotex
soap	sabuni
suntan lotion	dawa ya kukinga jua
tampons	OB/Tampax
talcum powder	poda
toothbrush	mswaki
toothpaste	dawa ya meno/Kolgeti

PHOTOGRAPHY

Film processing in East Africa is not always consistent. Some places are definitely better than others. The processing solutions in many places are often used over and over again, giving pictures an odd tint. In East Africa, they often use a red tint. If you don't want this, ask for rangi ya kawaida (no tint). You'll often be expected to pay in advance for film processing.

There are very few places that can repair a camera, especially the more complex models. Spare parts and the proper tools for camera repair are often lacking, although camera batteries are usually available in urban areas. Extra lens caps and lens protectors are a good idea. Many a lens cap has been lost on the bumpy roads through game parks and the countryside. You may want to bring a second 'back-up' camera if possible, though the more gear you have, the more tempting a target you are for thieves. For tips on picture-taking see page 87.

I need film.	Nahitaji filamu.
How much is it for ...?	Shilingi ngapi kwa ...?
Give me two rolls.	Nipe mikanda miwili.
Where can I get my film developed?	Je, kuna duka la kusafisha picha?
How much will it cost to develop the film?	Ni shilingi ngapi kusafisha picha?
When will it be ready?	Je, itakuwa tayari lini?
I'd like double prints.	Fanya kopi mbili mbili.
battery	betri
black & white film	filamu nyeusi na nyeupe

camera
  kemra

colour film
  filamu ya rangi

photo
  picha

roll of film
  mkanda wa filamu/picha

My camera is broken.
  Kemra ni mbovu.

Is there someone who can
  fix it?

Kuna fundikemra?

Where can I buy a camera?

Je, kuna duka lenye kemra?

JE ...?

The easiest way to indicate that you're asking a question is to start your sentence with the word je. It's used as if to say 'Hey, I'm asking a question.'

COLOURS

Many words for colours have a prefix that changes depending on the noun they are modifying. This requires a more advanced knowledge of the language. In this case, we recommend deferring to the 'n' class prefixes written below. You will have no problem being understood.

black	nyeusi
blue	buluu/samawati
dark blue	buluu iliyokoza
brown	kikahawia; rangi ya udongo
grey	rangi ya majivu/kijivu
green	rangi ya kijani
dark green	rangi ya kijani iliyokoza
light green	kijani kibichi
orange	rangi ya machungwa
pink	pinki
purple	zambarau
red	nyekundu
white	nyeupe
yellow	manjano

MATERIALS

If you want to describe the material that something is made from, use the word ya, 'of', before the name of the material – this will work for all the words in the list. For example, 'I'd like a wooden bowl', Nataka bakuli ya mti (lit: 'I want a bowl *of wood*').

bone	mfupa	leather	ngozi
clay	udongo wa kufinyanga	rubber	mpira
		silk	silki
copper	shaba	silver	fedha
cotton	pamba	stone	jiwe
gold	dhahabu	wood	mti
horn	pembe	wool	sufu

STATIONERY

I'm looking for a book about ...   Natafuta kitabu kuhusu ...
    the history of (Zanzibar)   historia ya (Zanzibar)
    the culture of (Kenya)   utamaduni wa (Kenya)
    the wildlife of (Tanzania)   wanyama wa (Tanzania)
    national and game parks   hifadhi ya nchi
    politics   siasa
    Swahili grammar   kitabu cha sarufi ya kiswahili

book	kitabu	newspaper/ magazine	gazeti
card	kadi		
dictionary	kamusi	paper	karatasi
envelope	bahasha	pen	kalamu

SHOPPING

flashlight	tochi	pencil	penseli
glue	gundi	scissors	mkasi
map	ramani	sticky tape	selo tepu

SMOKING

Acknowledgement of the evils of tobacco has not taken hold in East Africa, but fewer Africans than Europeans die of smoking because most can't afford more than the occasional cigarette. People buy cigarettes one by one when they have a little extra money. A visitor who shares tobacco with smokers will make many friends.

| Excuse me, do you have a light? | Tafadhali, una moto/kibiriti? |
| Do you smoke? | Wewe unavuta sigara? |

DID YOU KNOW ... African vultures have no sense of smell and so depend totally on their excellent eyesight, and that of their colleagues, for locating food. Once a kill has been sighted a chain reaction can sometimes bring these airborne scavengers from as far afield as 50km. It may be slim pickings for the late arrivals, however, because a large group of vultures (and they congregate in groups of up to 100) can strip an antelope to the bone in half an hour!

SHOPPING

You're welcome to a cigarette.
  Karibu sigara.
May I smoke here?
  Je, naweza kuvuta sigara
  hapa?
Please don't smoke.
  Usivute sigara hapa.
  Hairuhusiwi kuvuta sigara.
  Marufuku kuvuta sigara.
cigarettes
  sigara
tobacco
  tumbako
pipe
  kiko
match/matches
  kibiriti/vibiriti

'GA' WHAT!?

The suffix ga has no
known function but you'll
hear it used all the time.
Be aware that when it's
added it changes where
the stress in verbs
would normally fall.
Thus they will sound
different from what you
may be used to hearing.
Note the change of stress
between wanakula and
wanakulaga — they are
eating.

WEIGHTS & MEASURES

gram	grem/gremi
kilogram	kilogrem/kilogremi
pound	pauni
millimetre	milimita
centimetre	sentimita
metre	mita
kilometre	kilomita
half-litre	nusu lita
litre	lita
inch	inchi
foot	futi
yard	yadi
mile	maili

SIZES & QUANTITIES

The dashes before some adjectives indicate that they modify
according to the rules in the Adjectives section on page 37 of
the Grammar chapter. The most common form is the one shown
in brackets.

amount
   kiasi
a little
   kidogo
a little bit
   kidogo kidogo
a lot
   nyingi
enough
   bas/inatosha
too much/many
   mno
big
   kubwa

small	ndogo
heavy	-zito (nzito)
light	upesi
long	-refu (ndefu)
short	-fupi
tall	-refu (ndefu)

SHOPPING – CROSSWORD

Across

1. Inexpensive
3. Male traditional garb
5. Female traditional garb
7. Dental abrasion device
8. Cross between red and blue

Down

2. Sufficient
3. Material for writing on
4. Cap that fits neatly over bald spots
6. Easier and more useful to pass through the eye of a needle than a camel

Answers on page 223.

SHOPPING

Cuisine is rarely cited among the many reasons people visit East Africa but Zanzibar and the coast have fantastic seafood, often cooked in mild curries with coconut flavourings using locally grown spices. You can also find great restaurants in Nairobi. Elsewhere the story is different – restaurants offer little variety, meat is gristly, vegetables are only available seasonally and some travellers never get used to the staple ugali. You may need patience in your quest for a meal. You may even need the following phrases taken from an actual conversation at a rural hoteli (restaurant).

Is there food?	Je, kuna chakulua?
There's none.	Hamna.
Can you cook for us?	Unaweza kutupikia?
I can.	Naweza.
Then bring food.	Halafu lete chakula.
Sure, you're welcome to sit.	Sawa, karibu kukaa.

SHARING FOOD

While the food may not be what you're used to, eating with others forms the basis for social life in East Africa. When you do share a meal, don't be surprised if conversation stops while the food is being eaten – the usual practice is to pick up the conversation once everyone has finished eating and washed their hands.

There may be times when you have to refuse food, either because you're full or because you're served something you can't eat. If you don't eat meat, try to warn your hosts the moment they invite you to their home or to a meal. You'll avoid a great deal of embarrassment, you'll spare your hosts the expense of buying the meat and you may even spare the life of some hapless chicken. (More than a few travellers turn vegetarian when

FOOD

the morning's crowing alarm clock becomes the evening's stew!)
If necessary, you can invoke religious reasons as a diplomatic
solution to any such delicate social demands.

I don't eat meat.	Mimi sili nyama.
I'm vegetarian.	Nakula mboga tu.
I don't eat (goat/pig) meat.	Sili nyama (mbuzi/nguruwe).

WHEN VISITING ...

When visiting someone's home, it's usually expected that
you'll eat or drink something. If you want to leave but
suspect the women of the house may be preparing you
food, say:

Naomba niondoke.	I ask that I may leave.

You may be told:

Mama anapika.	The women are cooking.

or a woman cooking in the kitchen may call out:

Napika chakula.	I'm cooking food.

If you absolutely must leave, say:

Kweli, ni lazima niondoke.	Really, I have to go.

Your host may negotiate:

Kaa kidogo, kunywa chai.	Sit a little while and drink tea.

If you can, stay for tea, but explain that you must leave
soon:

Sawa, nitakunywa chai, halafu niondoke.	Okay, I'll drink tea and then I'll go.

It's because of my religion.	Ni kwa ajili ya dini yangu.
It's for health reasons.	Ni kwa ajili ya afya.
The doctor told me to quit.	Daktari aliniambia niache.

To avoid possible embarrassment, assume that a visit to someone's home, especially the first time, will extend into an offer of food.

FOOD

UGALI

While East African cuisine varies from region to region, most people will eat ugali – a traditional dish which is made by mixing maize or cassava flour (or a mixture of both) in hot water until it becomes stiff like bread. Ugali is then eaten with a sauce called mchuzi, containing either meat, fish, beans or spinach. If you go into a restaurant and use the phrase Lete chakula, 'Bring food', you'll get ugali.

Eating ugali with your hands is the quintessential East African culinary experience. When the food is ready, a pitcher of water and a bowl will be brought to the table for people to wash their hands. The ugali is served in one mound with bowls of mchuzi or mboga (vegetables or relish, again sometimes with meat) on the side. Each person pulls small lumps of ugali from their side of the mound with the right hand. Using the lump to fashion a kind of spoon, dip the ugali into the sauce, holding the meat, vegetables or beans with the thumb. Pop the whole thing into your mouth, then reach for another handful. If you start to get full, take smaller and less frequent handfuls. It's best to pace yourself so that everybody at the table finishes at about the same time. In private homes, stop while there's still a little ugali left in the bowl (unless you're still hungry!) – if you finish off the mound, your hostess will rush to prepare more because you're obviously not satisfied. When everyone has finished eating, your hostess will return with more water for people to wash their hands.

FOOD

If you're invited to a wedding, you might find yourself eating rice with your hands as though it were ugali. This is about the messiest meal you can imagine, but surprisingly tasty. The more reserved can always have their food served on a plate with a fork or spoon.

Should I bring a plate/spoon?	Nilete sahani/kijiko?
Thank you, I'm full.	Asante, nimeshiba.
I'm satisfied.	Nimetosheka.
Thanks for the food.	Asante kwa chakula.

water for washing hands	maji ya kunawa
drinking water	maji ya kunywa
sauce	mchuzi
vegetables	mboga

THEY MAY SAY ...

Karibu nyumbani.	Welcome to my home.
Karibu mpaka ndani.	Welcome inside (my home).
Karibu kukaa/kiti.	Have a seat.
Nawa mikono.	Wash your hands.
Karibu chakula.	Bon appétit. (welcome to food)
Karibu ugali.	Welcome to ugali.
Unajua kula na mikono?	Do you know how to eat with your hands?
Karibu tena.	Welcome again.
Karibu sana.	You're quite welcome.

FOOD

EATING OUT

The number of restaurants you come across will vary greatly, depending whether you are in cities or towns. European or Asian food can be found in regional capitals and touristed areas. Elsewhere, ask for a hoteli or mkahawa.

The word 'restaurant' has not entered the Swahili language, though enough tourists use the word 'restaranti' that you may be understood. Most large towns will have at least one restaurant where you can get Indian food, chakula cha kihindi. Unless you are at a fancy restaurant that caters for foreigners, prices will be cheap.

Is there a restaurant near here?	Je, kuna hoteli ya chakula hapo jirani?
I want European/Indian/ African food.	Nataka chakula cha kizungu/ kihindi/kiafrika.
Where's the restaurant?	Hoteli iko wapi?
Do you serve food here?	Mnauza chakula hapa?
I'd like …	Nataka …
I'll have prawn curry.	Nipe mchuzi wa praunsi.

Kuna mchuzi wa samaki na chapati.	There's fish curry with chapati.
Unahitaji kitu gani zaidi?	Something else?

Could you come here, please?	Tafadhali njo hapa; Ebu njoo.
Do you mind if I sit here?	(Je,) naweza kukaa hapa?
For (two) people.	Tupo (wawili).
One … (please).	Moja … (tafadhali).
I'm hungry/thirsty.	Nina njaa/kiu.
I'm full.	Nimeshiba/Nimetosheka.
This is delicious.	Chakula hiki ni kitamu.
This isn't very good.	Chakula hiki ni kibaya.
I don't eat meat.	Sili nyama.

FOOD

I eat eggs.	Nakula mayai.
I don't eat chicken.	Sili nyama kuku.
This food has too much hot pepper.	Chakula hiki kina pilipili kali mno.
I'd like a milder pepper.	Nataka pilipili isiyo kali sana.
Welcome/Join us!	Karibu!
Please come and have a drink.	Karibu kinywaji/pombe.
Which beverage/beer would you like?	Unataka kinywaji/bia gani?
Please eat.	Tafadhali kula.

TYPICAL DISHES

Mchuzi
sauce which can be made of any type of meat or available vegetable. Aside from coastal regions, people cook with few spices, so mchuzi can be fairly bland. You can spice it up with pilipili, hot peppers that are usually available.

Wali
cooked rice, is available in most restaurants with a variety of meats or sauces.

Chipsi
deep-fried potatoes (chips or french fries), are also commonly available as a main starch.

Chapati
a round bread cooked like a pancake. People usually tear off pieces of chapati and use it to pick up other foods.

Kande
a stew made with beans and whole kernels of maize. It's rarely served to foreigners, but it may well be available if you ask. If it's cooked well, with onions, it can be delicious.

Thank you, I'm full.	Nimeshiba, asante.
Please bring me the bill.	Nipe risiti tafadhali.
How much do I owe you?	Unanidai (shillingi) ngapi?
I'll pay! I invited you, you're my guest.	Nitalipa! Nimekualika wewe. Wewe ni mgeni wangu.

FOOD

If you manage to treat an East African guest, they'll usually want to return the favour in some way. If you accept another's treat, they'll often anticipate some reciprocal gesture of friendship, often a meal or gift of equivalent value.

TYPICAL DISHES

Chipsi mayai
an omelette made with chips. It's usually greasy, but tasty and satisfying, especially on the road. Ask for it kavu sana, 'very dry', or you might get gooey bits of uncooked egg.

Mkate wa mayai (lit: 'bread of eggs')
a mixture of eggs, ground meat, onions and spices, fried until brown. It's popular on the East African coast and is usually made while you wait because people like it hot.

Mishkaki
meat on a skewer, grilled to a crisp

Samosa or **sambusa**
a mixture of meat, onions, vegetables and spices fried in a triangular-shaped pastry, eaten as a snack.

Biriani and **pilau**
These Indian and Pakistani dishes (mixtures of rice and spices, usually with meat) have been adapted to East African tastes. As with most dishes, you can get biriani or pilau with goat meat, chicken, fish or beans.

FOOD

Useful Words

bowl	bakuli	salt	chumvi
cup	kikombe	spoon	kijiko
fork	uma	sugar	sukari
glass	bilauri	table	meza
knife	kisu	waiter	bwana/ndugu/
plate	sahani		mtumishi

Methods of Cooking

The word ya is perhaps not grammatically accurate in all the examples listed here, but it is simple and should work in most cases.

baked	ya kukaangwa
boiled	ya kuchemshwa
cooked/heated	ya kupikwa
fried	ya kukaangwa
not cooked	isiyopikwa
rare (meat)	(nyama) ya kuiva kidogo
raw	mbichi
ripe	mbivu
soft	laini
well done	ya kuiva kabisa/sana

DESSERTS

Desserts are not common in East Africa. People will serve you sweet food and hot tea, but usually *before* meal time. Biscuits and sweets sold by the roadside can be a bus passenger's salvation on long trips - ask for glukos, 'glucose biscuits'.

FOOD

biscuit/cookie	biskuti	gum	mpira/
bun (sweet)	swit/		bubble
	peremende	honey	asali
cake	keki	popcorn	popkon
candy	pipi	sugar	sukari

ROAD FOOD

Bus drivers make scheduled stopovers for food and fuel, and for people to make toilet stops. (It's often a better idea to go to the toilet, kujisaidia, (lit. 'help yourself') before your journey and avoid the filthy toilets at many roadside stops.)

> ### I Want ...
>
> Nipe , 'give me', lete , 'bring', nataka , 'I want', and naomba , 'I request', are all appropriate forms of address in the store. Though naomba can be more polite than necessary.

Roadside restaurants, however, usually have cheap, greasy food available relatively quickly. The menu is written on the wall but you can only be sure that a particular dish is available by asking. You'll usually find rice, meat, beans, chapati or mandazi, which will keep you going until your next stop. You can also buy fruit, hard-boiled eggs (mayai) and other food from vendors who come to the windows at each major bus stop.

If you are travelling by train, food is served in the buffet car but it can be expensive. Unless you've packed your own food, don't expect anything but sustenance from the food available en route. Avoid salads and unbottled drinking water on the road.

SELF CATERING

FOOD

I'd like …	Naomba …
Give me …	Nipe …
one can of …	mkebe/kopo moja wa …
one packet of …	paketi moja ya …
one box of …	boksi moja ya …
one kg of …	kilo moja ya …
half a kg of …	nusu kilo ya …
three …	tatu …

coffee	kahawa
cooking fat	kimbo (brand name)
cooking fat (flavoured)	mpishi (brand name)
cowpea (tropical pea)	kunde
curry powder	bizari
detergent powder	omo (brand name)
egg	yai/mayai (pl)
instant coffee	afrikafe
kidney beans	maharagwe
knife	kisu
lentils	dengu
maize (corn) meal	unga mahindi
margarine	blue bandi
matches	vibiriti
mung beans	pojo
oil	mafuta ya kupikia
paraffin (kerosene)	mafuta ya taa
pigeon pea	mbazi
powdered milk	maziwa ya unga
rice	mchele
salt	chumvi
spaghetti	spageti/makaroni
sugar	sukari
tea	chai
tinned (canned) meat	nyama ya mkebe/kopo
tinned (canned) sardines	samaki ya mkebe/kopo

tomato paste	tomato ya mkebe/kopo
tomato sauce	tomato (sos)
vinegar	siki

AT THE MARKET
Meat

Pork is considered haramu (prohibited) by Muslims and therefore often not sold at the butcher's. Because of a strong Muslim influence in East Africa, butchers are required to slaughter animals according to Islamic rules. Even non-Muslims will go to great lengths to find a Muslim to slaughter their meat.

beef/ox meat	nyama ng'ombe
chicken	nyama kuku
fish	samaki
goat	nyama mbuzi
lamb	kondoo
meat	nyama
offal	utumbo wa nyama; utumbotumbo
pork	nyama (ya) nguruwe

I'd like some beef.	Nipe nyama ya ng'ombe.
Two kg of fillet steak (please).	(Tafadhali) nipe kilo mbili ya sarara.
How much is a kilo of goat meat?	Kilo moja ya nyama ya mbuzi ni bei gani/shilingi ngapi?

Dairy Products & Eggs

butter	siagi
cottage cheese	jibini/chizi
cream (usually skim) from boiled milk	mtindi
eggs	mayai
margarine	blue bandi
milk	maziwa
yoghurt	maziwa ganda

FOOD

FOOD

Vegetables

Though usually translated from Swahili as 'vegetable', mboga is the generic term for all types of food that accompany rice, potatoes, cassava or ugali. Even meat is often called mboga when it's served with a main starch. At the market, though, you can be pretty certain that if you ask for mboga you won't be shown anything with blood in its veins.

beans	maharagwe	salad	saladi
cabbage	kabechi	spinach	mchicha
carrot	karoti	sweet potato	kiazi (itamu;
chilli (jalapeño)	pilipili		cha kienyeji)
corn/maize	mahindi	tomato	nyanya
onion	kitunguu	vegetable/	mboga/
potato	kiazi ulaya	vegetables	miboga

Fruit

apple	apol	mango	embe
avocado	embe mafuta	melon/	tikiti (maji)
banana	ndizi	watermelon	
dates	tende	orange	chungwa
fruit	tunda	papaya	papai
grapes	zabibu	(pawpaw)	
guava	pera	pineapple	nanasi
lemon	limau	sugar cane	muwa
mandarin	mandarini		

Herbs & Spices

Coastal residents, especially Muslims, use a great variety of spices. The most commonly used spice is pilipili (jalapeño-type chilly), which is served whole or sliced, or used as a powder.

black pepper	pilipili manga	coriander	giligilani
cardamom	iliki	cumin	kisibiti
cinnamon	dalasini	ginger	tangawizi
cloves	karafuu	turmeric	manjano

Legumes, Nuts & Pulses

almond	kungu	lentils	dengu
barley	shayiri	nut	nati
beans	maharagwe	pea	njegere
cashew	korosho	peanut	karanga
cowpeas	kunde	sunflower seeds	alizeti

DRINKS

It's common sense for travellers in East and Central Africa to boil tap water before drinking it. Some people store drinking water in jars or earthen jugs which they consider safe but sometimes there is no guarantee that the water has been boiled. Even rain water can be made unsafe because of the containers or the corrugated iron which is used to collect it.

Hot Drinks

People in East Africa drink tea and coffee all the time. On a hot afternoon it's not unusual to offer a visitor a thermos of prepared tea or coffee, often mixed with milk and sugar. It's different in Central Africa, where you could expect a cold drink, often a beer.

coffee	kahawa
black coffee	kahawa ya rangi;
	kahawa bila maziwa
coffee beans	kahawa isiyosagiwa
coffee pot	mdila
coffee with milk	kahawa ya maziwa
tea	chai
black	ya rangi
with lemon	na ndimu
with milk	ya maziwa
with spices	na tangawizi
with/without sugar	na/bila sukari

FOOD

milk (boiled)	maziwa (yaliochemswa)
milk (hot)	maziwa (ya moto)
hot cocoa	koko
hot water	maji ya moto

Cold Drinks - Nonalcoholic

If you want a drink to be cold, ask for it baridi. Even then soda baridi will only be as cool as the refrigerator or bucket of water it has been sitting in.

juice	jusi
fruit juice	jusi/maji ya matunda
lime juice	jusi/maji ya ndimu
orange juice	jusi/maji ya machungwa
pineapple juice	jusi/maji ya mnanasi
milk	maziwa
soda/soft drink (cold)	soda (ya baridi)
water (boiled/cold)	maji (ya kuchemka/baridi)
drinking water	maji ya kunywa
mineral water	maji safi

DID YOU KNOW ...

The usual samosa is ya nyama, 'with meat', so vegetarians should ask:

Je, kuna samosa bila nyama?
   Do you have samosas without meat?

Nipe ya bila nyama or Nipe enye haina nyama
   Give me one without meat.

Alcoholic Drinks

As well as spirits like whisky, there are different types of home-made brews, pombe. These vary depending on region, but the most common ones are made of maize, millet or banana. People near Kilimanjaro drink banana beer called mbege. Local brews are usually drunk from a shared plastic pot called a lita, though you can agree to pour from the pot into glasses, glesi. When joining a group of people drinking pombe, the accepted practice is to promptly order another litre which then gets added to the pot. By all means be tempted to partake of local brews, but be aware of the variety of intestinal parasites that may wind up partaking of you as a result.

Drinking is frowned upon in many Muslim areas, though visitors are usually catered for. In such areas travellers are expected to maintain decorum, limiting drinking and drunkenness to the bars and restaurants. On the other hand, drinking plays an important part in social life throughout most of East Africa. It's common for people to buy each other rounds of beer. You may find the waiter or bartender opening a beer sent to you by a friendly stranger. Though you are under no obligation, it's polite to eventually return the favour. Normally you should buy them a round unless you sense an unwelcome sexual advance.

Bring a litre of mbege (please).   Lete lita moja ya mbege
                                      (tafadhali).

alcoholic beverage	pombe
beer	bia
home brew	pombe ya kienyeji
ice	barafu
spirits	pombe kali
tonic	toniki
water	maji
whisky	wiski
wine	mvinyo

FOOD

Beer

Most East African people drink their beer warm. When you order, you should specify whether you want your beer cold or warm. Kenyan Tusker beer is called Taska in Kenya while in Tanzania it is called Ndovu. Safari beer has improved greatly in recent years, and is the only beer many Tanzanians will drink. Imported beers are often available – the Carlsberg from Malawi is especially nice. Usually you order beer by brand name. If you want to buy take-away, expect to leave a deposit for the bottles.

How much is the beer?	Bia ni bei gani?
Give me a cold beer.	Nipe bia baridi.
Please give me (3) Serengeti's.	Naomba Serengeti (tatu).
Should I open it?	Nifungue?
Yes, open it.	Ee, fungua.
Bring another round (please).	Ongeza (tafadhali).
cold beer	bia baridi
warm beer	bia ya moto

IN THE COUNTRY

ON SAFARI

Safari is the one common English word that is derived from Swahili. In Swahili it means a trip or journey of any kind; the verb kusafiri means 'to travel'. In English a safari is an adventurous trip, especially one to spot wild game. Hosting the safari business is extremely important to the economy of East Africa.

We're very keen to see ...	Sana sana tunataka tuone ...
Yesterday we saw ...	Jana tuliona ...
Today we saw ...	Leo tuliona ...
What's there?	Kuna nini pale?
What's that animal?	Huyo ni mnyama gani?

WILD ANIMALS

The Swahili word for animal is mnyama (wanyama, pl). Most animal names are the same in the singular and plural, but follow the grammatical forms for m/wa (animate) nouns discussed in the grammar section (see page 21).

Antelopes

antelope	pofu;kulungu; pala hala
bongo	bongo
bush duiker	funo/pofu
bushbuck	pongo/paa
dik-dik	dikidiki
duiker	funo/pofu
eland	pofu
gazelle	swala/swara/paa/impala
gerenuk	swala tiga
Grant's gazelle	swala granti
greater kudu	tandala mkubwa
hartebeest	kongoni

impala	swala/pala
klipspringer	mbuzi mawe
lesser kudu	tandala mdogo
oryx	choroa
reedbuck	tohe
roan antelope	korongo/kulungu
sable antelope	palahala
topi	nyemera/paa
waterbuck	kuru
wildebeest/gnu	nyumbu/mbogo

Birds

bird	ndege
flamingo	heroe
ostrich	mbuni
vulture	tai/gushu

BACK-TO-FRONT

Objects usually come after the verb, but you can put them the other way round to create emphasis,

eg We like meat.
   Tunapenda nyama.

or It's *meat* that we like.
   Nyama tunapenda.

Carnivores

cheetah	duma
civet	fungo
civet cat	ngawa
forest dog	mbwa mwitu
fox	mbweha
genet	fungo
	ngawa kanu
hyena	fisi
jackal	mbweha
leopard	chui
lion	simba
mongoose	nguchiro
serval	ngawa/mondo

Herbivores

buffalo	mbogo
camel	ngamia
elephant	ndovu/tembo

giraffe
  twiga
hippopotamus
  kiboko
hyrax; dassie
  pelele/kwanga
rhinoceros
  kifaru
warthog
  ngiri
water buffalo
  nyati
zebra
  punda milia

IN THE COUNTRY

Insects

army ants	siafu	mosquitoe(s)	mbu
centipede	tandu	spider	buibui
insect	mdudu		

Primates

baboon	nyani	monkey	tumbili
bushbaby	komba	vervet monkey	tumbili

Reptiles

crocodile	mamba	snake	nyoka
python	chatu	spitting cobra	swila

RURAL LIFE

beer club
  kilabu
board game with seeds
  bao
cattle pen
  boma
checkers
  draftsi

church	kanisa
crops	mazao
development	maendeleo
dispensary	dispensari
doctor of local medicine	mganga wa kienyeji
farm	shamba
farmer	mkulima
fertiliser (chemical)	mbolea (ya chumvichumvi)
health clinic	zahanati
hoe	jembe
house (brick/earthen)	nyumba ya (matofali/udongo)

HOME BREW

A kilabu, or 'beer club', is a little house where people gather to drink pombe ya kienyeji, 'local home brew', and to catch up on the latest gossip.

IN THE COUNTRY

manure	mbolea/samadi
market	soko
monthly market/auction	mnada
mosque	misikiti
ox plough	jembe la ng'ombe
path	njia
roof (metagrass thatch)	paa ya (bati/nyasi)
shop	duka/kioski
sub-village	kitongoji
village chairperson	mwenyekiti wa kijiji
village government	serikali ya kijiji
village office	afisi ya kijiji
village	kijiji
water pipe/tap	bomba la maji
worker	mfanyakazi

GEOGRAPHICAL FEATURES

bush	pori	countryside	porini
cave	pango	creek	mto
cliff	mwamba	desert	jangwe
coast	pwani	environment	mazingira

field	shamba	spring/well	kisima
forest	pori	stone/stones	jiwe/mawe
hill	kilima	swamp	bwawa
island	kisiwa	tree	mti
lake	ziwa	valley	bonde
mountain	mlima	waterfall	mporomoko
ocean	bahari		wa maji
river	mto		

IN THE COUNTRY

WEATHER

What's the weather like?	Hali ya hewa ikoje?
The weather's nice today.	Hali ya hewa ni nzuri leo.
The weather isn't good.	Hali ya hewa siyo nzuri.
It's (very) cold.	Ni baridi (sana).
It's (very) hot.	Ni joto (sana).

THEY MAY SAY ...

Hatari!	Danger!
Huyu ndiyo hatari.	This one's dangerous.
Hapana toka gari!	Don't get out of the car!
Usitoke gari!	
Baki garini!	
Ana watoto.	She has babies/pups/cubs.
Hapana sumbua!	Don't annoy it!
Usimsumbue!	
Tazama pale!	Look there!
Simba na watoto wake.	A lion and her cubs.
Ni mkali.	It's fierce.
Simba anawinda.	The lion's hunting.
kluza	Land Cruiser
rova	Land Rover
patroli	Nissan Patrol

It's dry.	Ni kavu.
It's raining.	Mvua inanyesha.
It's sunny.	Kuna jua.
It's windy.	Kuna upepo.
The sun's fierce.	Kuna jua kali.
Is it going to rain?	Mvua itanyesha?

biting wind	upepo kali
cloud/clouds	wingu/mawingu
drizzle	rasharasha
haze	kivumbi

DOMESTIC ANIMALS

bull	ng'ombe dume	goat	mbuzi
calf	ndama	guinea pig	simbalis
cat	paka	horse	farasi
chicken	kuku	mouse/rat	panya
cow	ng'ombe	pig	nguruwe
dog	mbwa	pigeon	njiwa
donkey	punda	rabbit	sungura
duck	bata	sheep	kondoo
cow	ng'ombe jike		

IN THE COUNTRY

IN THE COUNTRY – CROSSWORD

IN THE COUNTRY

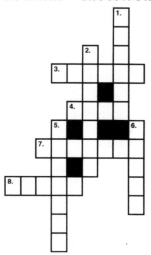

Across
3. Tract of land either cultivated or used to raise livestock
4. Carrion-eater with powerful jaws and a distinctive laugh
7. Flopsy, Mopsy and Cottontail were of this species
8. Reptilian chomper beloved by handbag aficionados

Down
1. Insect admired for its spinning skills
2. Airborne rainmakers
5. Distant relative of the human species
6. Do-it-yourself alcohol

Answers on page 223.

Most Tanzanian medical professionals speak fluent English, as that is the language in which they complete their studies. Although medical centres, pharmacies and doctors are located in all major towns, it's a good idea to carry a first-aid kit in more isolated areas.

Many visitors don't take their anti-malarial prophylactics as instructed by their physician. Remember to take them regularly — dying of totally preventable cerebral malaria can be a lousy end to an otherwise wonderful time in East Africa. If you get sick within the first month of your return home, insist that your physician give you an immediate malaria test.

Hygiene is very important while travelling in East Africa. Boiling drinking water, avoiding non-flowing water for swimming, and keeping clean are all important to ensuring you enjoy your time in East Africa.

If you find yourself needing medical help, try finding someone who can speak English. However, most medical terms are said as Swahili-ised versions of the English, so you should have little trouble communicating. For any ailments or conditions not listed here, use the English term.

Where can I find a (good) ...?	Naweza kupata ... (mzuri) wapi?
dentist	daktari wa meno
doctor	daktari/mganga
hospital	hospitali
medical centre	matibabu

AT THE DOCTOR

I'm sick.	Niko mgonjwa.
I'm in pain.	Naumwa.
My friend is sick.	Rafiki yangu ni mgonjwa.

My friend's in pain.	Rafiki yangu anaumwa.
I need a doctor.	Nataka kuona daktari.
I'm injured.	Nimeumia.
It hurts here.	Naumwa hapa.
That hurts.	Hapo panauma.
I'm feeling better.	Najisikia vizuri.
	Napona kidogo.
I'm feeling worse.	Najisikia vibaya zaidi.
I've been vaccinated.	Nimechanjwa.

THE DOCTOR MAY SAY ...

Kuna tatizo gani?	What's the matter?
(Je,) unaumwa?	Do you feel any pain?
Unaumwa wapi?	Where does it hurt?
Uko mwezini?	Are you menstruating?
Una homa?	Do you have a temperature?
Una maumivu haya kwa muda gani?	How long have you had this ailment?
Ni mara ya kwanza kuumwa hivi?	Is this the first time you've had this complaint?
Unatumia dawa?	Are you on medication?
Unavuta?	Do you smoke?
Unakunywa pombe?	Do you drink?
Kuna dawa ambayo hamsikilizani?	Are you allergic to anything?
Una mimba?	Are you pregnant?

HEALTH

AILMENTS

I feel dizzy.	Nasikia/Nasihi kizunguzungu.
I feel nauseous.	Nataka kutapika.
I feel shivery.	Natetemeka.

I feel weak.	Najisikia mnyofu.
I have (a/an) ...	Nina ...
anaemia	ukosefu wa damu
backache	umwa mgongo
bites (insect/dog)	nimeumwa na (mdudu/ mbwa)
breathing problems	pumua kwa shida
broken (leg)	nimevunjika (mguu)
burn	nimeungua
cold	baridi
constipation	funga tumbo
diarrhoea	harisha/hara/endesha
epilepsy	epilepsi
fever	homa
food poisoning	sumu ya chakula
headache	umwa kichwa
high blood pressure	shimikizo la damu
indigestion	tumbo linauma
itch	washwa
malaria	maleria
nausea/vomiting	tapika
rabies	nimeumwa na mbwa wa kichaa
skin disease	ugonjwa wa ngozi
sore throat	umwa koo
stomachache	umwa tumbo
sunburn	nimeungua na jua
toothache	jino linaniuma
venereal disease	ugonjwa wa usharti
vomiting	tapika
worms	mchango/vidudu
wound	kidonda
I've been bitten by a snake.	Niliumwa na nyoka.
I've been vomiting.	Nina tapika.
I can't sleep.	Siwezi kulala.

HEALTH

WOMEN'S HEALTH

I'm on the Pill.

Natumia vidonge vya
  kukinga mimba.

I think I'm pregnant. | Nadhani nina mimba.
I'm pregnant. | Nina mimba.
I want to see a female doctor? | Nataka kumwona daktari
  wa kike.

I haven't had my period
  for ... weeks.
Sijakwenda mwezeni
  kwa muda ya wiki ...
I'd like to use contraception.
Nataka kujikinga nispate
  mimba.

abortion
  kutoa mimba
contraceptive pill
  kuzuia mimba
menstrual pains
  maumivu ya mwezini
menstruation
  kwenda mwezini
miscarriage
  kutoa mimba
premenstrual tension
  maumivu ya kwenda
  mwezini

EASY ADJECTIVES

If you see an adjective
that begins with n, m, w,
k, ch, or v, it probably
changes prefixes to
agree with the class of
the noun it is being used
with. If you use n or m as
your prefix in such cases,
you'll usually be OK.

HEALTH

SPECIAL HEALTH NEEDS

I'm allergic to ... | Nina aleji ya ...
My friend is allergic to ... | Rafiki yangu ana alegi ya ...
  antibiotics | antibayotiki
  penicillin | penesilini

I have my own syringe. | Nina sindano yangu
  mwenyewe.

I'm on medication for ... | Nakunywa dawa ya ...
  asthma | ugonjwa wa pumu
  diabetes/epilepsy | dayabeti/epilepsi

PARTS OF THE BODY

ankle	kifundo
anus	mkundu
arm	mkono
back	mgongo
bone	mfupa
breast/breasts	
ziwa/maziwa;	
titi/matiti	
buttocks	
matako	
chest	
kifua	
ears	
masikio	
eye/eyes	
jicho/macho	
face	
sura/uso	
finger	
kidole	
fingernail/toenail	
kucha	
foot	
mguu	
hand	
mkono	
head	
kichwa	
heart	
moyo	
hip	
kiuno	
intestine	
utumbo	
knee	
goti	

HEALTH

leg	mguu	stool (faeces)	kinyesi
mouth	mdomo	teeth	meno
neck	shingo	testicle(s)	(ma)pumbu
nose	pua	throat	koo
penis	mboo	throat	koo
shoulder	bega	toe	kidole cha mguu
skin	ngozi	tongue	ulimi
spine	uti wa mgongo	vagina	kuma
stomach	tumbo	waist	kiuno

AT THE CHEMIST

Most pharmacists understand at least some English, but a proprietor of a rural duka la dawa, (lit: 'medicine shop'), may not have English skills beyond the names of the medicines. If you have no luck finding a teacher or someone else who speaks English, you can try using the 'Ailments' list on page 132 as a common reference point. You can usually buy sterile hypodermic needles, condoms and basic medicines such as aspirin and antibiotics without a prescription at any duka la dawa

I need something for …	Ninataka dawa ya …
I want two tablets.	Nataka vidonge viwili.
How many times a day?	Mara ngapi kwa siku?

pill	kidonge/vidonge (pl)
hypodermic needle/syringe	sindano
condom	kondom
aspirin	aspirini/panadol;
	dawa ya kichwa
antibiotics	antibayotiki
penicillin	penesilini

AT THE DENTIST

I've got a toothache.	Jino linauma.
I don't want it extracted.	Sitaki unitoe jino.
I want an anaesthetic.	Nataka anestetik.

AT THE OPTOMETRIST

I want my eyes checked.	Nataka kupimwa macho.
I'm long/short sighted.	Sioni mbali/karibu.
I need new glasses/ contact lenses.	Nahitaji miwani mipya/ kontakti lensi.

USEFUL WORDS

accident	ajali
addiction	uzowevu wa ulevi
AIDS	ukimwi
band-aid	plasta/elasto
bandage	kitambaa
blood group	aina ya damu
blood test	kupima damu
blood pressure	shindikizo ya damu
contagious	-a kuambukiza
contraceptive pill	kuzuia mimba
cream/ointment	dawa ya kupaka

DID YOU KNOW ... Zanzibar, or 'The Spice Island', has lured travellers to its shores for centuries, some in search of trade, some in search of plunder. The Sumerians, Assyrians, Egyptians, Phoenicians, Indians, Chinese, Persians, Portuguese, Omani Arabs, Dutch and English have all been there at one time or another.

HEALTH

faeces	mavi/kinyesi
(to have an) injection	(kupigwa) sindano
malnutrition	ukosefu wa chakula bora
medicine	dawa
menstruation	kwenda mwezini
patient	mgonjwa
poison	sumu
pregnancy	kuwa na mimba
sanitation	usafi
syringe	sindano/sirinji
urine	mkojo
virus	kirus/virus (pl)
vitamin	vitamini
water purifier	chombo cha kusafishia maji

HEALTH

TIME, DATES & FESTIVALS

TELLING THE TIME

The word for time, saa, also means 'hour', 'watch' and 'clock'. Time and hours are distinguished by different noun classes, so masaa mawili means 'two hours', while saa mbili (lit: 'the second hour') means '2 o'clock'.

What time is it?	Ni saa ngapi?
It's … o'clock.	Ni saa …
half past	na nusu
quarter past	na robo
quarter to	kasa robo
minute	dakika

The Swahili time system is quite different to what you're used to as it starts six hours later than the international clock system. The Swahili clock begins at sunrise which, close to the equator, occurs at about the same time each day all year round (6 am).

The first hour after sunrise is called saa moja (asubuhi), 'one o'clock (in the morning)', which corresponds to what we think of as 7 am. Counting continues until saa kumi na mbili (jioni) – '12 (in the evening)', which corresponds to 6 pm under the international system. After this, the clock begins again at saa moja (jioni), 'one o'clock (in the evening)'.

This system of time causes endless confusion for visitors to East Africa. Africans will sometimes try to accommodate your system when arranging plans, and if you are simultaneously trying to accommodate theirs, you can still end up missing appointments by six hours! To further confuse things, many people set their watches using the international system and then read them according to the Swahili system. Your best bet is to verify which system you are using – international time, saa za kizungu, or Swahili time, saa za kiswahili.

Since people usually specify what period of the day they are talking about, you can often determine which time system they are using from context.

International		Swahili clock
midnight	6	saa sita usiku
1 am	7	saa saba usiku wa manane
2	8	saa nane usiku wa manane
3	9	saa tisa usiku wa manane
4	10	saa kumi alfajiri
5	11	saa kumi na moja alfajiri
6 am (daybreak)	12	saa kumi na mbili asubuhi
7	1	saa moja asubuhi
8	2	saa mbili asubuhi
9	3	saa tatu asubuhi
10	4	saa nne asubuhi
11	5	saa tano asubuhi
noon	6	saa sita mchana
1 pm	7	saa saba mchana
2	8	saa nane mchana
3	9	saa tisa mchana
4	10	saa kumi mchana
5	11	saa kumi na moja jioni
6 pm (sundown)	12	saa kumi na mbili jioni
7	1	saa moja jioni
8	2	saa mbili usiku
9	3	saa tatu usiku
10	4	saa nne usiku
11	5	saa tano usiku
midnight	6	saa sita usiku

TIME, DATES & FESTIVALS

morning	asubuhi
afternoon	mchana
evening	jioni
night	usiku
very late at night	usiku wa manane
very early in the morning	alfajiri
daylight	mwanga
darkness	giza

It's 9 am.	Ni saa tatu asubuhi.
	(lit: It's-hour-three-night)
It's 2.45 pm.	Ni saa tisa kasa robo mchana.
	(lit: It's-hour-nine-minus-a quarter-afternoon)
It's 7.10 pm.	Ni saa moja na dakika kumi jioni.
	(lit: It's-hour-one-plus-minute-ten-evening)
Is it 10.15 am already?	Je, ni saa nne na robo tayari?

DAYS

Days of the week are very easy: Friday is the Islamic Sabbath day, so counting begins with Saturday (which uses a slightly unusual form of 'one'). Only Thursday and Friday diverge from the pattern.

day(s)	siku
week(s)	wiki

Saturday	Jumamosi
Sunday	Jumapili
Monday	Jumatatu
Tuesday	Jumanne
Wednesday	Jumatano
Thursday	Alhamisi
Friday	Ijumaa

DEAD POETS

It's more respectful to use the verb kufariki when speaking about a person who has died, and not kufa, which is used for animals, plants etc.

TIME, DATES & FESTIVALS

MONTHS

Swahili has two systems for counting months – mwezi/miezi (pl): the one that is easy for outsiders to remember and the one that Swahili speakers commonly use. We recommend you use the second system, which simply counts months as ordinal numbers (see page 150) with January conveniently coming first. At a pinch, though, many people will understand the English soundalikes.

January	Januari	mwezi wa kwanza (lit: month-first)
February	Februari	mwezi wa pili
March	Machi	mwezi wa tatu
April	Aprili	mwezi wa nne
May	Mei	mwezi wa tano
June	Juni	mwezi wa sita
July	Julai	mwezi wa saba
August	Agosti	mwezi wa nane
September	Septemba	mwezi wa tisa
October	Oktoba	mwezi wa kumi
November	Novemba	mwezi wa kumi na moja
December	Disemba	mwezi wa kumi na mbili

YEARS

Years are counted using cardinal numbers (see page 149). People usually use only the last two digits when speaking of years – mwaka/miaka (pl).

1961	mwaka (elfu moja mia tisa) sitini na moja (lit: 'year [thousand one hundred nine] sixty plus one')
1998	mwaka tisini na nane
1999	mwaka tisini na tisa
2000	mwaka elfu mbili
2001	mwaka elfu mbili na moja*

*There is no consensus about how to name years in the first decade of the 21st century - eg 2001.

TIME, DATES & FESTIVALS

DATES

Dates in months are given as ordinal numbers (see page 150), but without the intervening ya. As with days of the week, the unusual form, mosi, is used for 'one'.

date	tarehe
What's today's date?	Leo ni tarehe gani?
1 March	tarehe mosi, mwezi wa tatu
15 October	tarehe kumi na tano, mwezi wa kumi
Today is 17 June.	Leo ni tarehe kumi na saba, mwezi wa sita.
I leave on 7 December.	Naondoka tarehe saba, mwezi wa kumi na mbili.

PRESENT

today	leo	always	kila wakati
this week	wiki hii	every day	kila siku
this month	mwezi huu	just now	hivi sasa
this year	mwaka huu	now	sasa

DID YOU KNOW ... The black rhino is one of the poacher's most prized species. As a result they are now thought to number around 500, compared to around 20,000 in 1970. Numbers are now once again on the increase, thanks to determined conservation efforts.

TIME, DATES & FESTIVALS

PAST

yesterday	jana
day before yesterday	juzi
later	baadaye
long long ago	zamani
recently	hivi karibuni

last ...	... jana
week	wiki
month	mwezi
year	mwaka

FUTURE

tomorrow	kesho
day after tomorrow	kesho kutwa
not yet	bado
soon	sasa hivi

next ...	... kesho
week	wiki
month	mwezi
year	mwaka

SEASONS

Equatorial Africa has seasons, but they do not correspond to those of other parts of the world. Kiangazi is roughly June, July and August, which can be cold in the southern highlands of Tanzania, pleasant on the coast and hot in the northern regions of Kenya. Seasons vary greatly depending on altitude and latitude, so people may refer to the following seasons but have different times of year in mind.

rainy season	kipindi cha mvua
hot season	kipindi cha joto
cold season	kipindi cha baridi
harvest season	kipindi cha kuvuna

HOLIDAYS

East African nations observe a lot of holidays. In the effort to accommodate followers of Islam and Christianity, holy days of both religions are given national holiday status. Catholics are happy to take a day off work in commemoration of Id, while many Muslims will gather for a special meal on Christmas Day because it's a national observance. There are also days in honour of important events of national liberation; these are different in each country.

NEVER SAY NEVER

Bado is used to say 'no' in circumstances when it's theoretically possible the action may yet occur.

Have you climbed Kilimanjaro?	Umepanda Kilimanjaro?
Do you have children?	Umezaa watoto?/ Una watoto?
No, not yet.	Bado.

Sasa hivi translates as 'soon' or 'right away', but beware – 'soon' can sometimes be several hours away!

TIME, DATES & FESTIVALS

Variable   Holidays

Eid Al Fitr   Idilfitri
  usually celebrated in December or January

Good Friday   Ijumaakuu

Easter Monday   Pasaka
  Easter Saturday isn't a national holiday in Kenya

Eid Al Hajj   Idilhaj
  usually celebrated in March or April

Prophet's Birthday   Maulid
  usually celebrated in June or July

Hari Raya Puasa – generally in March (The sighting of the new moon signifies the first day of the Muslim calendar and the end of Ramadani, the fasting month.)

Fixed Holidays
Tanzania

12 January	Zanzibar Revolution Day	Sikukuu ya Mapinduzi ya Unguja
26 April	Union Day	Sikukuu ya Muungano
1 May	International Labour Day	Sikukuu ya Wafanyakazi
7 July	International Trade Fair Day	Sikukuu ya Sabasaba
8 August	Farmer's Day	Nanenane/Sikukuu ya Wakulima
9 December	Independence and Republic Day	Sikukuu ya Uuhuru
25 December	Christmas Day	Krismasi

Kenya

1 January	New Year's Day	Mwaka Mpya
1 May	Labour Day	Sikukuu ya Wafanyakazi
1 June	Madaraka Day	Siku ya Madaraka
10 October	Moi Day	Sikukuu ya Moi
20 October	Kenyatta Day	Sikukuu ya Kenyatta
12 December	Independence Day	Sikukuu ya Jamhuri
25 December	Christmas Day	Krismasi
26 December	Boxing Day	

Uganda

1 January	New Year's Day	Mwaka Mpya
6 February	Heroes' Day	Siku ya Zalendo

DID YOU KNOW ... Winston Churchill once referred to Uganda as the 'Pearl of Africa' but the country's long string of tragedies since independence in 1962 has featured in the western media to such an extent that most people probably still regard the country as dangerously unstable and to be avoided. The reality is very different. Stability has returned to most parts of the country, and Kampala is once again the modern bustling capital of Uganda with the fastest growing economy in Africa – the change has been astounding.

TIME, DATES & FESTIVALS

8 March	International Women's Day	Siku ya Wanawake
1 May	Labour Day	Siku ya Wafanyakazi
3 June	Ugandan Martyr's Day	Sikukuu ya Mashahidi
9 October	Independence Day	Sikukuu ya Jamhuri
25 December	Christmas Day	Krismasi
26 December	Boxing Day	

NUMBERS & AMOUNTS

CARDINAL NUMBERS

0	sifuri
1	moja
2	mbili
3	tatu
4	nne
5	tano
6	sita
7	saba
8	nane
9	tisa
10	kumi
11	kumi na moja
	(lit: ten-and-one)
12	kumi na mbili
13	kumi na tatu
14	kumi na nne
20	ishirini
21	ishirini na moja
	(lit: twenty-and-one)
22	ishirini na mbili
30	thelathini
40	arobaini
50	hamsini
60	sitini
70	sabini
80	themanini
90	tisini
100	mia or mia moja
200	mia mbili
	(lit: hundred-two)
300	mia tatu
1000	elfu

NUMBERS

2000	elfu mbili
	(lit: thousand-two)
10,000	elfu kumi
12,768	kumi na mbili elfu mia saba sitini na nane
	(lit: ten-and-two-thousand-hundred-seven- sixty-and-eight)
100,000	laki
hundreds	mamia
thousands	maelfu
one million	milioni
millions	mamilioni
one billion	bilioni

ORDINAL NUMBERS

Ordinals follow the object being counted. The words for 'first' and 'second' are different than the cardinal numbers. Ordinals follow the noun according to the rules for possessives discussed in the chapter on Grammar (see page 40), using a prefix + a. We recommend you use ya until you are comfortable with prefixes.

1st	ya kwanza	
2nd	ya pili	**GO KUKU!**
3rd	ya tatu	
4th	ya nne	Unlike verbs with more than one syllable, which drop their ku infinitive marker when they are conjugated, one-syllable verbs retain the ku when they are conjugated. Compare kula, 'to eat' – ninakula, 'I eat', and kusoma, 'to read' – anasoma, 'she reads'.
5th	ya tano	
6th	ya sita	
7th	ya saba	
8th	ya nane	
9th	ya tisa	
10th	ya kumi	
1000th	ya elfu	

1st time	mara ya kwanza
2nd trip	safari ya pili
12th night	usiku ya kumi na mbili

The following examples use the correct prefixes:

3rd child	mtoto wa tatu
5th book	kitabu cha tano
8th car	gari la nane

FRACTIONS

Fractions other than 1/2 and 1/4 are formed with the cardinal numbers. 1/3 is one (part) of three, and 4/5 is four (parts) of five.

half	nusu
a quarter	robo
three-quarters	robo tatu
a third	(sehemu) moja kwa tatu
	(lit: [part]-one-of-three)
two-thirds	(sehemu) mbili kwa tatu
four-fifths	(sehemu) nne kwa tano
nine-tenths	(sehemu) tisa kwa kumi

NUMBERS

DID YOU KNOW ... On Zanzibar the festival of Id al Fitr (the end of Ramadan) lasts about four days, and includes the Zanzibari equivalent of the tug-of-war where men from the south of the island engage in battle with those from the north by beating each other silly with banana branches. After a series of traditional folk songs performed by the women of the town, festivities then continue on into the small hours with much eating and dancing.

NUMBERS

USEFUL WORDS

Enough!	Inatosha!
It's not enough.	Haitoshi.
to count	-hesabu
decimal point	nukta
double/twice	mara mbili
dozen	kumi na mbili
equal	sawa
equal to	ni sawa na
few	chache
half (n, adj)	nusu
large	kubwa
little	ndogo
many	nyingi
minus	kasoro
much	nyingi
number (amount)	kiasi
number (numeral)	namba
once	mara moja
percent	asilimia
plus	na
some	kiasi
too much	mno
weight	uzito

EMERGENCIES

Stop!	Simama!
Help!	Nisaidie!/Saidia!/Njoo!/ Jamaani!
I need help!	Nipe msaada!
Emergency!	Ghafla!
Fire!	Moto!
Thief!	Mwizi!
Trouble!	Taabu!/Shida!
Please call the police!	Muite polisi tafadhali!
Could you please help me?	Tafadhali nisaidie. Je, unaweza kunisaidia?
Get an English speaker!	Fuata anayesema Kiingereza!
I need help.	Naomba msaada.
Could I please use the telephone?	Je, naweza kutumia simu yako?
It's an emergency.	Ni jambo la haraka.
There's been an accident.	Kulikuwa ajali.
I'm ill.	Naumwa.
Call a doctor!	Muite daktari!
I've been robbed!	Nimeibiwa!

SIGNS

POLISI	POLICE
KITUO CHA POLISI	POLICE STATION
HOSPITALI	HOSPITAL
ZAHANATI/DISPENSARI	CLINIC/DISPENSARY
HATARI!	DANGER!

EMERGENCIES

THAT'S THAT!

The easiest way to say 'this' or 'that' person or thing is to use these demonstrative pronouns:

People:

this	huyu	these	hawa
that	yule	those	wale

Things:

this	hii	these	hizi
that	hiyo	those	zile

That man drank this beer.
Yule bwana alikunywa bia hii.

I've lost my …	Nimepoteza …
backpack	mfuko wa kubeba mgongoni
bags	mifuko/begi
credit card	kredit kadi
glasses	miwani
handbag	mkoba
money	pesa/hela
passport	pasipoti
travellers cheques	cheki za kusafiri

Go away!	Toka!
Leave me alone!	Niache!/Usinisumbue!
I'll call the police!	Nitaita polisi!
I'm lost.	Nimepotea.

I'm sorry. I apologise.	Samahani. Naomba radhi.
I only speak English.	Nasema Kingereza tu.

Where is the nearest police station?	Kuna kituo cha polisi hapa karibuni?

DEALING WITH THE POLICE

I want to report a/an ...	Nataka kuripoti ...
accident	ajali
attack	kushambuliwa
loss	kupoteza vitu
theft	wizi
swindle/rip-off	unyang'anyi

I've been attacked.	Nimeshambuliwa.
I've been raped!	Nimenajisiwa!

I didn't do it.	Sikufanya.
I want to see a lawyer.	Nataka kuonana na mwanasheria.
I didn't realise I was doing anything wrong.	Sikujua kwamba ni kosa.
I wish to contact the (American) embassy/consulate.	Nataka kuonana na balozi wa (Marekani).

EMERGENCIES

THEY MAY SAY ...

Nionyeshe kitambulisho chako.	Show me your identification.
Umeshikwa na polisi.	You have been arrested.
Utalipa faini ya trafiki.	You're getting a traffic fine.
Nipe jina lako na anwani yako.	Give me your name and address.
Lazima twende kwenye kituo cha polisi.	You must come with us to the police station.
Nionyeshe ...	Show me your ...
pasipoti	passport
vitambulisho	identity papers
liseni ya kuendesha gari	driver's licence

EMERGENCIES

What's the charge?	Nashtakiwa nini?
Can I make a phone call?	Naweza kupiga simu?
I want an interpreter.	Nataka mkalimani/mtafsiri.

cell	lokap/jela
charge	mashtaka
complaint	malalamiko
(illegal) drugs	dawa (ya kulevya)
gun	bunduki/bastola
illegal possession of a weapon/ drugs	kuwa na silaha/dawa kinyume cha sheria
knife	kisu
police station	kituo cha polisi
thief/thieves	mwizi/wezi
theft	uizi/kuibiwa
weapon	silaha

This vocabulary section should help you through many situations. For an up-to-date Swahili-English dictionary, we recommend you download the free *Internet Living Swahili Dictionary* at http://www.yale.edu/swahili.

The words and phrases in this section were selected for their combination of ease of use and accuracy. In many cases, Swahili speakers may use other terms to convey the same meaning. We hope the phrases we selected here are adequate for all your needs, but please let us know if there is vocabulary you think should appear in future editions.

We show most verbs and many adjectives in their stem form – i.e., stripped of any of the prefixes that describe the action of the verb or the subject of the adjective. For a detailed explanation, please read through the relevant sections on page 22 in the Grammar chapter. Many words that are adjectives in English are adjectival phrases in Swahili; for example, the literal translation of -enye baridi kidogo which we use for 'cool', is 'with a little cold'.

When you see the word -enye or -a, refer to the following chart for the correct form to use in 'survival' Swahili sentences:

one person	mwenye	wa
two (or more) people	wenye	wa
one thing	yenye	ya
two (or more) things	zenye	za

A

(to be) able -weza
May I (have permission to) take your photo?
Naomba (ruhusa) kupiga picha.
Can you show me on the map?
Unaweza kunionyesha kwenye ramani?
aboard kwenye
(a boat/plane) (ndege/meli)
abortion -toa mimba
(to have an)
about kuhusu/juu ya

above juu ya
abroad nchi za nje
absolutely kabisa
to accept -kubali
accident ajali
accommodation mahali pa kulalia
ache maumivu
across ng'ambo
addiction uzowevu wa ulevi
address anwani
administration utawala

to admire	-penda sana	air	hewa/upepo
admission	ruhusa ya kuingia	air-conditioned room	chumba kwenye a/c
to admit	-kubali	airline	kampuni ya ndege
adult	mtu mzima		
advantage	faida	air mail	kwa ndege
adventure	jambo la kubahatisha/ kujihatarisha; ujasiri	airport	kiwanja cha ndege
		airport tax	ushuru wa usafiri
advice	shauri	alarm clock	saa ya kuamsha
to advise	-shauri	alcohol	pombe kali
aeroplane	ndege	all	yote
afraid	kuwa na uwoga	allergy	aleji
		to allow	-ruhusu
after(wards)	baadaye	It's allowed.	
afternoon	mchana	Inaruhusiwa.	
this afternoon	mchana huu	almost	karibu
again	tena	alone	peke yake
to lean/be against	-egemea	already	tayari
age	umri/iaka	also	pia
aggressive	mkali	altitude	kimo; urefu juu ya bahari
(a while) ago	(muda) uliopita		
half an hour ago	nusu saa iliopita	always	saa zote; kila wakati
three days ago	siku tatu zilizopita	amazing	ya ajabu
		ambassador	balozi
to agree	-kubali	among	katika; kati ya; baina ya
I don't agree.			
Sikubali.			
Agreed! (we agree)		ancestors	akina babu
Tunakubaliana!/Sawa!		ancient	kale
agriculture	kilimo	and	na
ahead	mbele	animal	mnyama
to aid	-kusaidia		(pl wanyama)
aid	msaada	to annoy	-sumbua
aid organisation	mradi wa msaada	annual	kila mwaka
		another	-ingine
AIDS	ukimwi	to answer	-jibu

answer (n)	jibu	asthmatic	mwenye pumu
ant	siafu	at	kwa/katika
antibiotics	antibiotiki	atmosphere	hali ya hewa
antiques	vitu vya kale	aunt	shangazi
antiseptic	antiseptik;	(father's sister)	
	dawa ya	awful	mbaya sana
	vijidudu		
any	yoyote	**B**	
anything	kitu chochote	baby	mtoto mchanga
apart	mbali	baby food	chakula cha
appointment	mkutano		mdogo
approximately	kiasi/	baby powder	poda ya mtoto
	kama/	babysitter	yaya
	hivi	back	mgongo
archaeology	maarifa ya	back (behind)	nyuma
	mambo ya	bad	mbaya
	kale	bag; backpack	mfuko
architect	mjuzi wa ujenzi	baggage	mizigo
architecture	ujenzi	Baggage Claim	Mizigo
to argue	-bishi	baker	mwokaji
arid	kavu		(mikate)
arm	mkono	bakery	duka la mkate;
arrivals	wanaofika		bekri
to arrive	-fika	balcony	baraza
art	sanaa	ball	mpira
art gallery	nyumba ya	banana	ndizi
	sanaa	band (music)	bendi/kikundi
artist	mwanasanaa	bandage	plasta/
artwork	sanaa		kitambaa
as	kama	bank	benki
ashtray	sahani ya	banknote	noti
	majivu	baptism	ubatizo
ask	-uliza	bar	baa
to ascend	-panda	to bark	-bweka
to be ashamed	-ona haya	basket	kikapu/
aspirin	dawa ya kichwa;		kitunga
	aspirini;	bath	bafu
	panadol	to bathe	-oga
asthma	ugonjwa wa pumu		

B

D
I
C
T
I
O
N
A
R
Y

159

bathing suit	nguo za kuogolea
bathroom (shower)	bafuni
bathroom (toilet)	choo
battery	betri
bay	ghuba
to be	kuwa
beach	pwani/ ufuoni/ ufukwe
beans	maharage (maharagwe)
beard	ndevu
beautiful	-zuri
because	kwa sababu
bed	kitanda
bedbug	kunguni
beef	nyama ya ng'ombe
beer	bia/pombe
before	kabla ya
beggar	mwombaji
to begin	-anza
beginner	mwanafunzi nyuma
behind	-amini
to believe	
bell	kengele
below	chini
to bend	-pinda/-inama
beside	pembeni
best	nzuri kabisa/ sana
better	nzuri zaidi; bora
to get better (from sickness)	-pona
between	katikati
the Bible	Biblia

bicycle	baisikeli
big	kubwa
binoculars	darubini
bird	ndege
birth certificate	cheti cha kuzaliwa
birthday	siku kuu ya kuzaliwa
biscuit	biskuti
to bite	-uma
to be bitten	-umwa
bitter	chungu
black	-eusi
to blame	-laumu
blanket	blanketi
to bleed	-toka damu
to bless	-bariki
Bless you. (when sneezing) Afya, Mungu akubariki.	
blind	kipofu
blister	lengelenge
blonde	mzungu mwenye nywele nyeupe rangi ya kimanjano
blood	damu
blood pressure	shimikizo la damu
blood test	pima damu
blood type	aina ya damu
to blow	-vuma
blow	pigo/dharuba
blue	buluu
board	mbao
board (ship, etc)	-panda
boarding pass	cheti cha usafiri

boat	boti/meli
body	mwili
to boil	-chemsha
bomb	bomu

Bon appétit!
Karibu chakula!
Bon voyage!
Safari njema!

bone	mfupa
book	kitabu
to book	-fanya buking
bookshop	duka la vitabu
boots	buti
border	mpaka
to be bored	-choka
boring	ya kuchosha
to be born	-zaliwa
to borrow	-azima

Please may I borrow your …
Tafadhali, naweza
kuazima … yako?

boss	bosi
both	yote mbili
bottle	chupa
bottle opener	kifuli
bottom	chini
box	boksi
boy	mvulana
boyfriend	mpenzi
bracelet	bangili
branch	tawi
brand	aina
brave	shujaa
bread	mkate
to break	-vunja/-pasua
breakfast	chai cha asubuhi
breast	titi
to breastfeed	-nyonyesha
to breathe	-pumua
breeze	upepo

bribe	rushwa
bridge	daraja
bright	ya kung'aa; angavu
to bring	-leta
to be broken	-vunjika
brother	kaka
brown	rangi ya kahawa
bruise	chubuko
bucket	ndoo
bug	mdudu
to build	-jenga
building	jengo
bulb	kioo cha taa ya umeme
bull	ng'ombe dume; fahali
to burn	-choma
bus (small)	daladala (Tanz)/ matatu (Kenya)
bus (large)	basi
bus stop	kituo cha basi
bush country	porini
business	shughuli/ biashara
business person	fanyabiashara
to be busy	-shughulika
but	lakini
butcher	mwuuza nyama; bucha
butter	siagi
butterfly	kipepeo
buttons	vifungo
to buy	-nunua

I'd like to buy …
Nataka kununua …

by	karibu na; kwa; na

C

cabbage	kabeji
café	mgahawa/mkahawa
calendar	ratiba
to call	-ita
camera	kemra
camp	-piga hema; -kempi

Can we camp here?
Tunaweza kupiga hema hapa?

campsite	mahali pa kukempi/ kupiga hema
can; tin	mkebe/kopo
can (to be able)	-weza
can-opener	kifunguo cha kopo/mkebe
candle	mshumaa
canned	ya mkebe; ya kopo
capitalism	ukapitalisti/ ubepari
car	gari/motokaa
cards (playing)	karata
to care (about)	-jali

I don't care. (it doesn't matter)
Mimi sijali.

to take care of	-tunza
careful	angalifu

Careful!
Angalia!
Be careful!
Uwe mwangalifu!

to carry	-beba
cashier	mshika fedha; kashia
cassava	mhogo
cassette	kanda

cat	paka/pusi
to catch	-shika/ -chukuwa
Catholic	romani
cattle	ng'ombe
cave	pango
to celebrate	-sherekea
cemetery	kaburi
cent	senti
centimetre	sentimita
centre	katikati
certain	hakika
certificate	cheti
chair	kiti
chairperson	mwenyekiti
chance	nafasi/bahati
change (cash)	chenji
to change	-chenji;
money	-badili pesa
to change (trains)	kubadili (treni)
charcoal	mkaa
to chat	-zungumza/ -ongea
cheap	bei rahisi
cheap hotel	gesti
to cheat	-dang'anya

You cheated me!
Umenidang'anya!

to check	-kagua
checkpoint	kizuio
chemist	duka la dawa
cheque	cheki
chewing-gum	mpira/babol
chicken	kuku
chief	chifu
chief of police	mkuu wa polisi
child	mtoto (pl watoto)
chilled	ya baridi
to choose	-chagua
to chop	-kata

(a) Christian	mkristu
Christmas	Krismasi
church	kanisa
cigarettes	sigara
cinema	sinema/filamu
circle	mviringo
citizen	mwananchi/raia
citizenship	uraia
city	mji
class (school)	darasa
1st class (seat)	(kiti cha) daraja la kwanza
2nd class	daraja la pili
3rd class	daraja la tatu
to clean	-safisha

This room isn't clean.
  Chumba hiki si kisafi.

clever	janja
client	mteja
cliff	mwamba
to climb	-panda
clock	saa
close (near)	karibu
to close	-funga

The store is closed.
  Duka limefungwa.

cloth	kitambaa
clothes	nguo
clothing store	duka la nguo
cloud	wingu
cloudy	kuna mawingu
coast	pwani
coat	koti
coconut	dafu
coffee	kahawa
coins	chenji
cold (temp.)	baridi

It's cold.
  Ni baridi.

cold (illness)	mafua/ ugonjwa

I have a cold.
  Mimi ni mgonjwa.

cold water	maji baridi
colleague	mwenzi
college	chuo kikuu
colour	rangi
comb	kichanuo
to come	-ja

Come!
  Njoo!

comfortable	starehe
common (customary)	ya kawaida
communion	komunio ya kwanza
communism	komunism
his/her companion	mwenzake
my companion	mwenzangu
your companion	mwenzako
company	shirika/ kampuni
compass	dira
computer	kompyuta
comrade	ndugu
concert	muziki
condom	kondom
conductor	kondakta
to confess	-kiri
to confess (religious)	-ungama
to confirm	-hakikisha
congratulations	hongera
to be constipated	-funga tumbo
construction work	ujenzi
contagious	-enye kuambukiza
contraceptive	kuzuwia mimba
contract	mkataba
conversation	maongezi/ mazungumzo

convict	mfungwa/mahabusi
to cook	-pika
cook (n)	mpishi
cool	-enye baridi kidogo
cool (slang)	safi
cooperative	ushirika
corn; maize	mahindi
corner	kona/pembe
to correct	-sahihisha
correct (adj)	sahihi/sawa
correction	adhabu/maonyo
to corrupt	-toa rushwa; -potoa; -haribu
corruption (n)	ubovu/rushwa
cost (n)	bei
How much does it cost?	
Ni bei gani?	
cotton	pamba
to cough	-kohowa
cough (n)	kikohozi
to count	-hesabu
country	nchi
coup d'etat	mapinduzi wa serikali
court (legal)	mahakama
courtyard	uwanja
cousin	binamu
cow	ng'ombe
crab	kaa
crafts	vitu vya sanaa
craftsman	fundi
crafty	mjanja
cramp	maumivu
crazy	-enye kichaa
cream	maziwa ya mtindi
credit card	visa kadi; american express kadi

creep (slang)	mhuni
crocodile	mamba
crop	zao
cross (n)	msalaba
to cross	-vuka
crowded	enye watu wengi; umati wa watu
to cry	-lia
cry (n)	mlio
to cuddle	-bembeleza
to cultivate	-lima
cup	kikombe
cupboard	kabati
current affairs	habari za kisasa
customs (traditions)	mila na desturi
customs (border)	forodha
customs duty	ushuru
to cut	kata
to cycle	-endesha baisikeli

D

dad	baba
daily	kila siku
dairy (products)	(ya) maziwa
damp	unyevu
dance	ngoma
(with traditional drums)	
to dance	-cheza densi
danger	hatari
dangerous	ya hatari
dark	giza
date (time)	tarehe
to date (person)	-tongoza
date of birth	tarehe ya kuzaliwa
daughter	binti

164

dawn	kucha/alfajiri
day	siku
day after tomorrow	kesho kutwa
day before yesterday	juzi
in (six) days	baada ya siku (sita)
dead	amekufa
(she/he is dead)	
deaf	ziwi
deaf (person)	kiziwi
death	kifo/mauti
to decide	-amua; -kata shauri
decision	maamuzi
deep	-refu
deforestation	upungufu wa misitu
degree (university)	digrii/ shahada
to delay	-chelewesha
We were delayed.	
Tulicheleweshwa.	
delicious	tamu/nzuri
delightful	ya kufurahisha sana; ya kupendeza sana
delirious	-payuka
democracy	demokrasi
demonstration (university)	maandamano
dentist	daktari wa meno
to deny	-kataza
to depart	-ondoka/-enda
Departures	
Wanaoondoka	
depth	kina
descendant	bin
desert	jangwa/nyika

design	rasimu
destination	kifiko/mahali
to destroy	-haribu/-vunja
detail	kila kitu; habari yote
development	maendeleo
dial tone	sauti ya simu
to have diarrhoea	-harisha/ -endesha
I have diarrhoea.	
Naharisha.	
diary	kumbukumbu
dictatorship	dikteta; mtawala kwa nguvu peke yake
dictionary	kamusi
to die	-fa/-fariki
I'll die if we keep going.	
Nitakufa tukiendelea.	
(Our child) died.	
(Mtoto) amefariki.	
She/he has left this world.	
Amefariki dunia.	
Sorry for the death (of your child).	
Pole kwa kufiwa (mtoto).	
different	tofauti; mbali mbali
difficult	-gumu
dinner	chakula cha usiku
direct	moja kwa moja
to direct	-ongoza/ -elekeza
dirt	uchafu/udongo
dirty	chafu
disabled	kilema
disadvantage	hasara
to discount	-punguza bei
to discover	-gundua/ -vumbua

E

discrimination	ubaguzi/ upambanuzi
disease	ugonjwa
disinfectant	dawa ya kuondoa uchafu wa kuambukiza ugonjwa
distant	ya mbali
dizzy	kizunguzungu
to do	-fanya

What are you doing?
Unafanyaje?
I didn't do it.
Sijafanya.

doctor	daktari/mganga
dog	mbwa
doll	mtoto wa bandia
door	mlango
dope	bangi/hashishi
double	mara mbili
double room	chumba cha watu wawili
double bed	kitanda cha watu wawili
downstairs	chini
downtown	mjini
dream (n)	ndoto
to dress	-vaa nguo
dry	kavu
to dry	-kauka
drink (n)	kinywaji
to drink	-nywa
drinkable (water)	(maji) ya kunywa
to drive	-endesha
driver's licence	laiseni (ya kuendesha gari)
drugs (medicine)	dawa
drugs (illicit)	dawa ya kulevya

to be drunk	-lewa
drunkard	mlevi
during	wakati wa; katika; kwa
dust	vumbi/unga

E

each	kila
ear	sikio (pl masikio)
to be early	-wahi

It's early.
Ni mapema.

to earn	-pata/-chuma kwa kazi
earnings	mshahara/ chumo
earrings	hereni
earth (soil)	ardhi/udongo
Earth	dunia
earthquake	mtetemeko wa nchi
east	masbariki
easy	rahisi
to eat	-la

Have you eaten yet?
Umekula tayari?
I've already eaten.
Tayari nimekula.

economical	ni rahisi
economy	uchumi
editor	mtengenezaji
education	elimu/mafunzo
elder	mzee
to elect (vote)	-piga kura
election	uchaguzi
electricity	umeme
elevator (lift)	lifti
embarrassment	aibu/haya
embassy	ubalozi

emergency	ghafla
employee	mfanyakazi
employer	mwajiri
empty	wazi
end (n)	mwisho
to end	-maliza
energy	nguvu; uwezo wa kufanya kazi
engine	injini
English person	Muingereza
English (language)	Kiingereza
to enjoy (oneself)	-jifurahisha
to enjoy	-furahia
enough	ya kutosha
Enough! Inatosha!	
to enter	-ingia
entry	mlango
envelope	bahasha
environment	mazingira
epilepsy	kifafa/ kifundofundo
equal	sawa/ sawasawa
equality	umoja
equipment	vifaa
European	mzungu
evening	jioni/ magharibi
event	tokeo/tukio
every	kila
every day	kila siku
everyone	kila mtu
everything	kila kitu
exactly	kamili
example	mfano
for example	kwa mfano
to exchange	-badili/ -badilisha
Excuse me!	Samehani!

to be exhausted	-choka sana
to exhibit	-onyesha
exile	ukimbioni
to exit	-ondoka
exotic	-geni
expensive	ghali
experience	maarifa/ uzoefu
to export	-uza vitu nchi za nje
express	ekspres
eye	jicho (pl macho)

F

face	sura/uso
factory	kiwanda
false	ya uwongo
family	jamaa/familia
famous	maarufu
fan	feni
far	mbali
How far is ...? ... ni umbali gani?	
farm	shamba
farmer	mkulima
to fast	-funga
fast (quick)	haraka/upesi
fat	mafuta
fat person	mnene
father	baba
father-in-law	babamkwe
to fatten	-nenepa
fault	kosa
my fault	kosa langu
to fear	-ogopa
fee	malipo/ada
to feel	-hisi/-ona
feelings	maono
female	ya kike; mwanamke
fence	wigo

ferry	meli cha kuvushia watu	foot	mguu
		football	soka/mpira
festival	sikukuu/karamu	footpath	njia ya miguu
fever	homa	for	kwa; kwa kuwa
few	chache	foreign	ya kigeni; ya nchi nyingine
fiancé/e	mchumba		
field	shamba	forever	kwa milele; hata milele
fight (n)	pigano/vita		
to fight	-pigana/ -gombana	to forget	-sahau
		I forget.	
to fill	-jaza	Nimesahau.	
film	filamu ya; sinema	Forget about it. (don't worry) Usijali.	
film (roll of)	mkanda ya kemra	to forgive	-samehe/ -wia radhi
		formal	rasmi
filtered water	maji yaliosafishwa	fortune teller	msibu
		fragile	ya kuvunjika upesi; dhaifu
find	-kuta		
fine (penalty)	faini		
finger	kidole (pl vidole)		
fire	moto	free (of charge)	bure
firewood	kuni	free (not bound)	huru
first	kwanza	to freeze	-ganda
first-aid	huduma ya kwanza	fresh (not stale)	ya sasa
		Friday	Ijumaa
fish	samaki	fried	ya kukaangwa
flag	bendera	friend	rafiki
flashlight (torch)	tochi	friendly	ya pole; ya wema; nzuri
flea	kiroboto		
my flight	ndege yangu		
flood	furiko la maji; gharika	from	kutoka/tokea/ tangu
		fruit	tunda
floor	sakafu	full (it's full)	imejaa
floor (storey)	ghorofa	full stop (period)	nukta
flour	unga	to have fun	-furaha
flower	ua (pl maua)	to make fun of	-tania
fly	-ruka	funeral	kilio
to follow	-fuata	funny	ya kuchekesha
food	chakula	future	mbeleni; siku zijazo
food poisoning	sumu ya chakula		

G

game	mchezo
	(pl michezo)
game (sport)	metchi
garbage	takataka
garden	bustani
gas (petrol)	petroli
gate	mlango wa nje
gay	msenge
generous	karimu
Get lost!	
Toka! Niacha!	
girl	msichana;
	mtoto wa kike
girlfriend	mpenzi
to give	-pa/-toa
Give me ...	
Nipe ...	
I'll give you ...	
Nitakupa ...	
glass (of water)	bilauri/gelasi
	(ya maji)
glasses/	miwani
spectacles	
to go	-enda
I'm going to ...	
Nakwenda ...	
Let's go.	
Twende.	
Go straight ahead.	
Endelea moja kwa moja.	
to go out with	-tongoza
goat	mbuzi
God	Mungu
gold	dhahabu
good	-ema/safi/
	-zuri
Good afternoon.	
Habari za mchana.	
Good evening.	
Habari za jioni.	

Good luck.	
Bahati njema.	
Good morning.	
Habari za asubuhi.	
Good night.	
Usiku mwema.	
Goodbye.	
Kwa heri/Tutaonana.	
government	serikali
gram	gramu
grandchild	mjukuu
grandfather	babu
grandmother	bibi
grass	nyasi
grave (n)	kaburi
greedy person	mlafi
green	rangi ya majani
grey	rangi ya majivu
to grow	-mea
to guess	-bahatisha
guide (person)	mwongozi
to guide	-ongoza
guidebook	kitabu cha
	mwongozo/
	maelezo
guilty	kosefu;
	-enye dhambi
guinea pig	simbalis
guitar	udi/gitaa

H

hair	nywele
hairbrush	kichanuo
half	nusu
hammer	nyundo
hammock	machela
hand	mkono
handbag	mkoba/begi
handicrafts	sanaa; kazi ya
	mikono

handmade	ya mikono
handsome	mzuri
happy	-enye furaha
to be happy	-furahi

Happy birthday.
Heri za sikukuu. (lit: blessings
on your holiday)

harbour	bandari
hard	-gumu
harrassment	usumbufu
to hate	-chukia
to have	kuwa na
I have	nina
you have	una

Have you (got) ...?
Una ...?

head	kichwa

I have a headache.
Naumwa kichwa.

health	afya
hear	-sikia
heart	moyo
heat	joto/moto
heavy	-zito
Hell	Jehenamu

Hello!
Habari!

Hello. (answering telephone)
Halo.

help (n)	msaada
to help	-saidia
here	hapa
high	-refu/juu
high school	sekondari
to hike	-tembea mlimani
hiking boots	buti ya kupandia milima
hill	kilima
to hire	-ajiri/ -panga

I want to hire it.
Nataka kuipanga.

to hitchhike	-omba lifti
She/he is HIV positive.	Ana kirus cha ukimwi.
holiday	sikukuu/livu/ likizo
holy	takatifu
home	nyumbani
homeland	nchi/makao
homeless	bila nyumba; bila mahali
homesick	hamu ya urudi nyumbani
homosexual (n)	msenge (pl wasenge)
honest	mwaminifu
honey	asali
to hope	-tumaini
horse	farasi
hospital	hospitali
hospitality	ukarimu
hot	joto/moto

It's hot.
Ni joto.

hotel	gesti/hoteli
house	nyumba
housework	kazi ya nyumbani
how	njia gani; namna gani

How do you get to ...?
Ni njia gani kufika ...?

How do you say ...?
Unasemaje ...?

How much?
Kiasi gani?/Wauzaje?

How much to ...?
Ni bei gani mpaka ...?

to hug	-kumbatiana

human	kibinadamu
to be hungry	-wa na njaa
I'm hungry	
Nina njaa	
Are you hungry?	
Una njaa?	
to be in a hurry	-wa na haraka;
	-harakisha
hurt	umiza/uma
husband	mume;
	bwana;
	baba watoto

I

I	mimi
ice	barafu
idea	wazo/fikara
ID (card)	kitambulisho
idiot	mjinga
if	kama/ikiwa
to be ill	-sikia mgonjwa;
	-ugua
illegal	kinyume cha
	sheria
imagination	mawazo/akili
imitation	mwigo/uigaji/
	ufuasi
immediately	sasa hivi;
	papa hapa
immigration	uhamiaji
to import	kuingiza vitu
	kutoka nchi
	za nje
important	muhimu;
	ya maana
It's important.	
Ni muhimu.	
It's not important.	
Siyo muhimu/ya maana.	
(it's) impossible	haiwezikani

imprisonment	kifungo/
	kufungwa
in	katika/ndani/
	kwa
in a hurry	kwa haraka
in front of	mbele ya
included	ndani yake;
	pamoja
income tax	kodi ya mapato
incomprehensible	haieleweki
inconvenient	sumbufu/
	isiyofaa
indigestion	tumbo linauma
indoors	ndani ya
	nyumba;
	ndani
industry	kiwanda
infection	ambukizo
infectious	ya kuambukiza
informal	isiyo ya rasmi
information	habari/taarifa
injection	dawa ya
	sindano
injury	maumivu/
	jeraha
insect repellent	dawa ya
	kufukuza
	wadudu
inside	ndani; ndani ya
instant	mara moja;
	kwa ghafla
instructor	mwalimu
insurance	bima
I have health/travel insurance.	
Nina bima ya afya/usafiri.	
to insure	-fanya bima ya
It's insured.	
Ina bima.	
intelligence	akili/busara

to be interested	kupendezwa/ kuvutiwa
interesting	ya kupendeza; ya kuvuta
international	ya kati ya mataifa
interview	mahojiano
to invite	-alika/ -karibisha
island	kisiwa
to itch	-washa
itch (n)	upele/ukurutu
itinerary	ratiba

J

jail (gaol)	gereza/ kifungo
to jail (someone)	-funga gerezani
jar	mtungi
to be jealous	-ona wivu
jewel	johari
jewellery	vipuli
job	kazi
joke (n)	mzaha/soga
I'm joking.	
Nafanya mzaha.	
journalist	ripota
journey	safari
judge	hakimu
juice	jusi
to jump	-ruka
jumper (sweater)	sweta
justice	haki/usawa

K

key	ufunguo
to kick	-piga teke
to kill	-ua
kilogram	kilo
kilometre	kilomita

kind (n)	aina
kind (adj)	-enye huruma; karimu
king	mfalme
kiss	busu/kisi
kitchen	jiko
kitten	kipaka
knapsack	mkoba/mfuko
knee	goti
kneel	piga goti
knife	kisu
to know (a person)	-fahamu
know (s'thing)	-jua
I don't know.	
Sijui.	

L

lake	ziwa
lamp	taa
land	ardhi
landslide	mtelemko wa ardhi
language	lugha
large	kubwa
last (adj)	ya mwisho
last month	mwezi uliyopita
last night	jana usiku
last week	wiki jana; wiki iliyopita
last year	mwaka uliyopita
What time does the last boat leave?	
Meli ya mwisho itaondoka saa ngapi?	
late	ya nyuma; ya mwisho
to be late	-chelewa
later	baadaye
to laugh	-cheka
laugh (n)	cheko/kicheko

laundry woman/man	dobi
law	sheria
lawyer	mwana sheria
lazy	vivu
leader	mwongozi
learn	jifunza/ kusoma
I'm learning Swahili. Najifunza/Nasoma Kiswahili.	
leather	ngozi
left (not right)	kushoto
to be left (behind, over)	-baki
leg	mguu
legal	halali; ya haki
legislation	sheria
lesbian	shoga
less	dogo zaidi; chache zaidi
letter	barua
liar	mwongo
library	maktaba
lice	chawa
to lie	-sema uwongo
life	maisha/uhai
lift (elevator)	lifti
light	mwanga
to light (a fire)	-washa
light (clear)	-eupe
light (not heavy)	nyepesi
light bulb	globu
lighter	kriket
like (similar)	kama/sawa
to like	penda
I like ... Napenda ...	
line	mstari
lips	midomo

listen	sikia/ sikiliza
little; small	-dogo
little (amount)	-chache
a little bit	kiasi
to live (be alive)	-ishi
to live (s'where)	-kaa
local	kienyeji
local (city) bus (Kenya)	matatu
local (city) bus (Tanz)	daladala
location	mahali
lock (n)	kifuli
to lock	-funga
long	-refu
long ago	zamani sana; zamani za kale
long-distance/ international call	simu kutoka mbali/kutoka nchi ya nje
long-distance bus	basi ya kusafiri mbali
to look at	-tazama/ -angalia
to look for	-tafuta
I'm looking for ... Natafuta ...	
to lose (a game)	-shindwa/ poteza
to lose (object)	-poteza/-kosa
loser	aliyeshindwa
to be lost	-potea
a lot	nyingi
loud	kwa sauti kubwa
love (n)	upendo
to love	-penda
to love each other	-pendana

I love it.
Na(i)penda.
I love you.
Nakupenda.

lover	mpenzi
low	chini
luck	bahati
lucky	-enye bahati
luggage	mizigo
lunch	chakula cha mchana
luxury	anasa/starehe

M

machine	mashine
mad (crazy)	kichaa
madman	kichaa
to be made of	-tengenezwa na; -fanywa na
magazine	gazeti
mail	barua/posta
mailbox (PO Box)	sanduku la posta (SLP)
main road	barabara kuu
majority	waliowengi
to make (create)	-tengeneza
man	mwanaume (pl wanaume)
manager	bosi/mkuu
manual work	kazi ya mkono
many	-ingi

Many happy returns!
Heri na hongera!

map	ramani

Can you show me on the map?
Unaweza kunionyesha kwenye ramani?

marijuana	banghi
market	soko
marriage	ndoa
to marry (for a woman)	-olewa
to marry (for a man)	-oa
marvelous	ya ajabu
mass	misa
mat	mkeka
match/matches	kibiriti/vibiriti
material	kitambaa

It doesn't matter.
Siyo kitu.
What's the matter?
Una shida gani?

mattress	godoro
maybe	labda/pengine
mayor (of village)	mwenyekiti (wa kijiji)
mechanic	fundi
medicine	dawa
to meet	-kuta; -kutana na
to meet for the first time	-fahamiana

I'll meet you.
Nitakukuta.

member	mwanachama
menstrual pains	maumivu ya kwenda mwezini
menstruation	kwenda mwezini
menu	orodha ya vyakula
message	ujumbe
metal	chuma
meter	mita
midnight	saa sita usiku
military	jeshi/kijeshi
milk	maziwa
millimeter	milimita
million	milioni

mind (n)	akili/fikra/busara
minister	mchungaji
minute	dakika
Just a minute.	
Nipe dakika moja.	
in (five) minutes	
baada ya dakika (tano)	
mirror	kioo
to miscarry	-toa mimba
to miss (feel absence)	-kumbuka
miss (bus, etc)	-kosa
mistake	kosa
to mix	-changa/-changanya
mobile phone	selfon
modern	ya kisasa; siku hizi; mpya
monastery	seminari
money	fedha/pesa/hela/shilingi
month	mwezi
this month	mwezi huu
monument	nguzo ya kumbukumbu
moon	mwezi
more	zaidi/tena
morning	asubuhi
mosque	misikiti
mosquito	mbu
mosquito coil	sumu ya mbu
mosquito net	chandarua
mother	mama
mother-in-law	mamamkwe
motorboat	mashua
motorcycle	pikipiki
mountain	mlima
mountain bike	baisikeli kwenye gia
mountaineering	kupanda milima
mountain path	njia ya kupanda mlimani
mouse	panya
mouth	mdomo
movie	filamu
mud	udongo
muscle	musuli
museum	makumbusho
music	muziki
musician	mwanamuziki
Muslim	mwislamu
Mr.	Bwana
Mrs.	Bi
mute	bila sauti; kimya

N

name	jina
What's your name?	
Jina lako nani?	
My name is …	
Jina langu ni …	
national park	mbuga ya wanyama
nationality	uraia
natural resources	mali asili
nausea	hali ya kutapika
near	karibu/jirani
necessary	lazima
necklace	mkufu
to need	-hitaji
needle (sewing)	sindano (ya kushona)
needle (syringe)	sindano (ya dawa)
neither	wala
net	neti

net (mosquito)	chandarua	often	mara nyingi
never	kamwe	oil (cooking)	mafuta ya
new	-pya/mpya		kupikia
news	habari/taarifa	oil (lamp)	mafuta ya taa
newspaper	gazeti	oil (motor)	mafuta ya gari
	(pl magazeti)	OK	sawa/haya
next	ya kufuata;	old	-zee; ya kale
	ya pili	old city	mji mkangwe
next bus	basi	old person	mzee
	inayofuata	(respected elder)	
next month	mwezi ujayo	on	juu ya
next to	pembeni	to be on time	-wahi
next week	wiki ijayo;	once	mara moja tu
	wiki kesho	one	moja/mosi
nice	-zuri	one-way ticket	tikiti ya
nice person	mtu mwema		kwenda tu
nickname	jina la	only	tu
	kudangwa	to open	fungua
night	usiku	What time does it open?	
noise	kelele	Watafungua saa ngapi?	
noisy	-enye kelele	open (adj)	wazi;
none	sifuri;		-enye
	hata moja		kufunguliwa
north	kaskazini	operation	udaktari wa
nothing	si kitu		kupasua
not yet	bado	operator	opereta
novel (book)	kitabu cha	opinion	maoni
	hadithi	opportunity	nafasi/wakati
now	sasa	opposite	kinyume
nurse	mwuguzi/nesi	or	au/ama
		orange (fruit)	chungwa
O		orange (colour)	rangi ya
			machungwa
obvious	wazi/dhahiri	order (n)	agizo
occupation	kazi/shughuli	to order	-agiza
ocean	bahari	ordinary	ya kawaida
to offend	-chukiza	organisation	chama/shirika
to offer	-toa/-tolea	to organise	-panga
office	afisi/ofisi	to orgasm	-fika
officer	afisa	original	ya asili
office work	kazi ofisini	other	nyingine

ENGLISH – SWAHILI

out	nje
outside	nje
over	juu; juu ya
overcoat	koti
overnight	usiku mpaka asubuhi
overseas	nchi za nje

to owe – The verb 'to owe' is actually the passive form of -dai, 'to claim'. 'I owe you' can either be expressed by Unanidai, 'You claim from me', or by Nadaiwa, 'I am claimed by you". Or try: kuwa na deni; -daiwa.

I owe you. (lit: I have your debt)
Nina deni lako.
You owe us. (lit: You have our debt)
Una deni letu.

owner	mwenye/ mwenyewe
oxygen	hewa/oksijeni

P

package	furushi
pack of cigarettes	paketi ya sigara
packet	paketi
padlock	kufuli
page	ukurasa
painful	ya kuumiza
pain in the neck	sumbufu
painkillers	dawa ya maumivu
pains	maumivu
to paint	-paka rangi
pair	jozi

We're a couple.
Tupo pamoja.

pan	sufuria
paper	karatasi
paraplegic	kilema
parcel	kifurushi/ bahasha
parents	wazazi/ wazee
park	bustani/ hifadhi
to park a car	-paki
parliament	bunge
Member of Parliament	mbunge
part	sehemu/ kipande
to participate	shiriki
participation	ushirika
particular	maalum
party (celebration)	sherehe/ karamu
to party (celebrate)	-sherehekea
party (political)	chama
multi-party elections	uchaguzi wa vyama vingi
to pass	-pita
passenger	abiria
passport	pasipoti
passport number	namba ya pasipoti
past	zamani
path	njia
patient (adj)	mvumilivu
to pay	-lipa
payment	malipo
peace	amani
peak	kilele
pen	kalamu/bik
pencil	kalamu/ penseli
penknife	kisu

P

DICTIONARY

people	watu	planet	sayari
pepper	pilipili	to plant	-panda
... percent	asilimia ...	plant (n)	mmea
perfect	kamili/halisi	plastic	plastiki
period (full stop)	nukta	plate	sahani
permanent	daima;	play (theatre)	mchezo wa
	ya siku zote		kuigiza
permission	ruhusa	to play	-cheza
permit	cheti cha	to play cards	-cheza karata
	ruhusa;	player (sports)	mchezaji
	ruhusa	playing cards	karata
persecution	mateso/fukuzo	please	tafadhali
person	mtu	to please	-furahisha
personal	binafsi	plenty	wingi/tele
personality	utu	pocket	mfuko
to perspire	-toka jasho	poetry	shairi
petition	maombi	to point	onyesha
petrol	petroli		(wa kidole)
pharmacy	duka la dawa	police	polisi
phone	simu	political speech	hotuba
photo	foto/picha	politician	mwanasiasa
to photograph	-piga picha	politics	siasa
May I take a photograph?		pollution	uchafu
Naomba kupiga picha.		pool (swimming)	bwawa
photographer	mpiga picha	poor	maskini/
to pick up	-chukua/-okota		fukara
piece	sehemu/	positive (certain)	ya hakika
	kipande	to be possible	-wezekana
pig	nguruwe	it's not possible	haiwezikani
pill	kidonge	postcard	postkadi
	(pl vidonge)	post office	posta
the Pill	kidonge cha	port	bandari
	kuzuia mimba	pot (ceramic)	chungu
pillow	mto	pot (dope)	banghi
pillowcase	foronya	poverty	umaskini/
pipe	bomba		ufukara
place	mahali	power	nguvu
place of birth	mahali pa	practical	ya kufaa;
	kuzaliwa		ya kutumika
plane	ndege/	prayer	sala
	eropleni	to prefer	-pendelea

preferable afadhali
(to be) pregnant (kuwa) na mimba
to prepare -tayarisha
to prepare food -andaa chakula
present (gift) zawadi
present (time) ya kisasa; siku hizi
president rais
pressure shindikizo
pretty ya kupendeza
  You look pretty!
  Unapendeza!
to prevent -zuia
price bei
  Can you lower the price?
  Je, unaweza kupunguza bei?
pride fahari/majivuno
priest padre
prime minister waziri mkuu
prison gereza/ jela/ kifungo
prisoner mfungwa
private binafsi
private hospital hospitali binafsi
probably labda/ huenda
problem tatizo/ shida/ taabu
process njia/ harakati
procession andamano
to produce -tengeneza
produce (n) mazao/ mavuno
professional mtalamu
profit faida/ mapato
program mradi

promise (n) ahadi
to promise -ahidi
proposal mapendekezo
to propose -pendekeza
prostitute malaya/ kahaba
to protect -linda/ -tunza/ -hifadhi
protected forest hifadhi ya misitu
protest (n) mandamano
public ya watu wote; ya jamii
to pull -vuta
pump (water) bomba
puncture pancha
to punish -adhibu
puppy mbwa mdogo
pure halili/ halisi
purple zambarua
push sukuma; endesha mbiyo; himiza
to put -weka

Q

qualifications ujuzi
quality sifa
quarantine karantini
quarrel ugomvi
to quarrel -gombana
one quarter robo
question swali
to question -uliza
quick -epesi/ upesi
quiet kimya
to quit -acha

R

rabbit	sungura
race (contest)	shindano
race (colour)	rangi
racism	ubaguzi wa rangi
racist	mbaguzi wa rangi
radio	redio
railroad	treni; gari la moshi
railroad station	stesheni ya treni
rain	mvua

It's raining.
  Mvua inanyesha.

to rape	-najisi
rare	adimu
rash (n)	upele/ ukurutu
rat	panya
rate of pay	mshahara
raw	-bichi
razor	wembe
to read	-soma
ready	tayari
to realise	-tambua
reason	sababu
receipt	risiti
to receive	-pokea
recently	hivi karibuni
to recognise	-baini/ -tambua
to recommend	-pendekeza
recording (music)	kanda (ya musiki)
red	nyekundu
referee	mwamuzi
refrigerator	friji
refugee	mkimbizi
to refund	-rudisha pesa

to refuse	-kataa
region	mkoa
to regret	-juta
regulation	sheria
relation	jamaa/ ndugu
relationship	uhusiano
to relax	-starehe
religion	dini
religious person	mtu wa dini
to remember	-kumbuka
remote (distant)	mbali
rent (n)	kodi
to rent	-kodi/ -panga
to repeat	-rudia

(Could you) repeat that.
  Sema tena.

representative	mjumbe
republic	jamhuri
reservation	buking
to reserve	-fanya buking; -weka akiba
to resign	-jiuzulu
respect	heshima
respected person	heshimiwa
responsibility	daraka
rest (relaxation)	pumziko/ raha
to rest	-pumzika
rest (remainder)	inayobaki
restaurant	mkahawa/ hoteli
results	matokeo
to retire	-staafu
to return	-rudi/ -rejea
return (ticket)	(tikiti) ya kwenda na kurudi

revolution	mapinduzi
rhythm	mahadhi
rich	tajiri
Rift Valley	Bonde la Ufa
right (not left)	kulia
right (not wrong)	haki/ sawa

You're right.
Una haki.

civil rights	haki ya uraia
right now	sasa hivi
ring (on finger)	pete

I'll ring you.
Nitakupigia simu.

to rip-off, chisel	-punja
risk	hatari
river	mto
road	barabara/ njia
main road	barabara kuu
road map	ramani
to rob	-iba
robber	mwizi

I was robbed!
Niliibiwa!

rock	jiwe (pl mawe)
romance	mapenzi
roof	paa
room	chumba
room number	namba ya chumba
rope	kamba
round	mviringo/ duara
roundabout	kiplefti
round trip	kwenda na kurudi
rubbish	takataka
ruins	maghofu
rule	kanuni/ sheria
to rule	-tawala
to run	-kimbia

S

to be sad	-sikitika
sadness	huzuni
safe (n)	sefu
safe (adj)	salama
to have safe sex	-jikinga; -vaa kondom
safety	salama/usalama
saint	mtakatifu
salary	mshahara
salt	chumvi
salty	yenye chumvi
same	ile ile; kile kile; sawa; yule yule
sand	mchanga
sanitary napkin	Kotex (etc) (known by brand names)
Saturday	Jumamosi
to save	-okoa
to say	-sema
to scale (climb)	-kwenda juu
scenery	sura ya nchi
school	shule
secondary school	sekondari
primary school	shule ya msingi
science	sayansi
scientist	mwanasayansi
to score	-piga goli
sculptor	mchongaji; mchoraji
sculpture	mchongo/ mchoro
sea	bahari
seasick	kutapika wakati wa usafiri

seaside	pwani	shade; shadow	kivuli
seat	kiti	shape	umbo
seatbelt	kamba	to share	shiriki/
second (not first)	ya pili		gawa
secret	siri	to shave	-nyoa
secretary	karani/katibu	she	yeye
to see	-ona	sheep	kondoo
We'll see!		sheet (bed)	shuka
Tutaona!		sheet (paper)	ukurasa
I see (understand).		shell	gome
Naelewa.		ship	meli
See you later.		to ship	-posta
Baadaye.		shirt	shati
See you tomorrow.		shoe	kiatu (pl viatu)
Tutaonana kesho.		to shoot	-piga risasi
selfishness	umimi	shop	duka
to sell	-uza	to shop	-enda
to send	-tuma/		mudukani
	-peleka	short (time)	kipindi;
sensible	-enye busara;		muda mfupi
	-enye akili	short (height)	fupi/-dogo
sentence	kifungo	shortage	upungufu
(prison)		shorts	kaptura
sentence	sentensi	shoulder	bega
(words)		to shout	-piga kelele
to separate	-tenga	show (n)	maonyesho
series	mafuatano/	to show	-onyesha
	mfululizo	Show me.	
serious	mzito/	Nionyeshe.	
	ya maana	shower	bafu
service	huduma/	shower	bafuni
(assistance)	msaada	to shut	-funga
service	misa	shyness	aibu/haya
(religious)		to be sick	-sikia
several	kadhaa		mgonjwa;
to sew	-shona		-ugua
sex (f/m)	ya kike/	sickness	ugonjwa
	ya kiume	side	upande
to have sex	-lalana	sign (posting)	kibao
sexist	mbaguzi wa	sign (symbol)	dalili/
	jinsi		alama

182

to sign	-weka sahihi; saini
signature	sahihi
silver	fedha
to be similar	-fanana
simple	rahisi
sin	dhambi
since (May)	tangu/tokea (Mei)
since (because)	kwa sababu ya
to sing	-imba
singer	mwimbaji
single (unique)	pekee; peke yake

I'm single.
Ni peke yangu.

single room	chumba cha mtu moja
sister	dada
to sit	-kaa/ -keti
situation	hali
size	kiasi/ saizi
skin	ngozi
sky	hewa
sleep (n)	usingizi
to sleep	-lala; -sinzia; -lala usingizi
to be sleepy	-sikia usingizi; -choka
slide film	salaidzi
slow/slowly	polepole/ taratibu

Slow down! (to a driver)
Endesha polepole!
Punguza mwendo!
Slow down! (to someone speaking)
Sema polepole!

small	-dogo/ kidogo
smell (n)	harufu
to smell (bad)	-nuka
to smell (good)	-nukia
to smile	-tabasamu

Smile!
Tabasamu!

smoke (n)	moshi
to smoke (cigarettes)	-vuta (sigara)
sneeze	piga chafya
soap	sabuni
soccer	soka
social science	sayansi ya jamii
socialism	usoshalizm/ ujamaa
society	jamii
solid	gumu/ imara
some	baadhi
somebody	fulani; mtu moja
something	kitu/ jambo
sometimes	mara kwa mara; pengine
son	mvulana
song	wimbo (pl nyimbo)
soon	karibu

I'm sorry.
Pole.

sound	sauti
south	kusini
souvenir	ukumbusho/ kumbukumbu
space (room)	nafasi
space (outer)	mbingu
to speak	-sema

Do you speak English?
Je, unasema Kiingereza?
I can speak Swahili.
Nasema Kiswahili.
I can't speak Swahili.
Sisemi Kiswahili.

spear	mkuku
special	maalum
specialist	mtaalamu
specific	maksusi
speed	mwendo
spicy	pilipili

I (don't) like it spicy.
Napenda (Sipendi)
chakula chenye pilipili
nyingi.

sport	mchezo
to sprain	-teguka
square (shape)	pembenne
square (town center)	uwanja
stadium/ sports field	uwanja wa michezo
stairs	ngazi
stamp	stempu
standard (usual)	ya kawaida; kanuni
standard of living	hali ya maisha
star	nyota
to start	-anza
station	stesheni
statue	sanamu
statute	sheria
to stay (remain)	-baki
to stay (s'where)	-kaa
to steal	-iba
steam	moshi
steep	mlima mkali
stomach	tumbo
stomachache	tumbo linauma

stone	jiwe
to be stoned (drugged)	-lewa kwa dawa
stop (bus, etc)	kituo/stendi
to stop	-simama

Stop here.
Simama hapa.

storm	dharuba
story (tale)	hadithi
straight	moja kwa moja
strange	ya ajabu; ya kigeni
stranger	mgeni
stream	mto
street	njia
strength	nguvu
a strike	mgomo
string	uzi
stroll	-tembea
strong	enye nguvu
stubborn	kichwa ngumu
to be stuck	-kwama/ -kwamisha
student	mwanafunzi
stupid person	mjinga/ mpumbavu
style	mtindo/ namna/ jinsi
suburb	kijiji jirani ya mji
to succeed	-faulu
success	mafanikio
suddenly	ghafla
to suffer	-hangaikia/ -teseka
sugar	sukari
suitcase	mzigo
sun	jua
sunblock	dawa ya kukinga jua

sunburn	kuchomwa na jua
sunglasses	miwani ya jua
It's sunny.	
Kuna jua.	
sunrise	mashariki
sunset	magharibi
suntan lotion	dawa ya kukinga jua
sure	hakika
Sure.	
Sawa.	
surface (by boat) mail	kwa meli
surname	jina la pili
surprise (n)	ajabu
to surprise	-staajabu/ -shangaza
I'm surprised.	
Nashangaa.	
to survive	-zidi kuishi; -salimika
Swahili	Kiswahili
I can speak Swahili.	
Nasema Kiswahili.	
I can't speak Swahili.	
Sisemi Kiswahili.	
sweet (adj)	tamu
sweet (n)	peremende
sweet person	mtu mtamu; mtu mwema
to swim	-ogolea
swimming pool	bwawa ya kuogolea
swimsuit	nguo ya kuogolea
sword	panga
sympathetic	mwenye huruma
synagogue	kanisa ya kiyahudi

syringe	sindano

T

table	meza
to take	-chukua
to take pictures	-piga picha
tale	hadithi
to talk	-sema/ -ongea/ -zungumza
tall	mrefu
tampons	OB (etc)
(known by brand names)	
tasty	ladha (nzuri)
tax	kodi
taxi	teksi
taxi stand	stendi ya teksi
to teach	-fundisha
Teach me.	
Nifundishe.	
teacher	mwalimu
team	timu
tears (crying)	machozi
to tear/rip	-pasua
technique	mbinu
teeth	meno
telegram	telegramu
telephone (n)	simu
to telephone	-piga simu
telephone book	kitubu kwenye namba za simu
telephone office	telecom
(in Dar, Nairobi)	
television	televisheni
to tell	-ambia
temperature (fever)	homa
temperature (weather)	temperecha; hali ya hewa

test (n)	mtihani	together	pamoja/
to test	jaribu		wote/
to thank	-shukuru		jumla
Thank you.		toilet	choo
Asante/Shukrani.		Where are the toilets?	
Thanks.		Choo kiko wapi?	
Shukrani.		toilet paper	karatasi ya
there	hapo/pale/		choo
	kule/huko/	tomorrow	kesho
	mle/humo	tomorrow	kesho mchana
they	wao	afternoon	
thick	nene	tomorrow	kesho jioni
thief	mwizi (pl wezi)	evening	
thin	mwembamba	tomorrow	kesho asubuhi
to think	-fikiri/	morning	
	-dhani	tonight	usiku huu;
I don't think so.			leo usiku
Sidhani.		too (also)	pia
to be thirsty	-wa na kiu;	too	mno
	-sikia kiu	(many, much)	
thought	fikra/	tooth	jino (pl meno)
	wazo	toothache	maumivu ya
throat	koo		jino
ticket	tikiti	toothbrush	mswaki
ticket office	ofisi ya tikiti	toothpaste	dawa ya meno
tide	mawimbi	torch (flashlight)	tochi
(to be) tight	-bana	total/totally	kabisa
time	saa/	to touch	-gusa
	muda/	tour	safari ya kutalii
	wakati	tourist	mtalii
to be on time	-wahi	toward	kwa;
What's the time?			kwenye pande
Ni saa ngapi?			wa
timetable	ratiba	towel	taulo
tin (can)	mkebe	town	mji
tip (gratuity)	zawadi/	track (path)	njia
	bakshishi	track (footprints)	nyayo
to be tired	-choka	trade union	ushirika wa
toast	slaisi		wafanyakazi
tobacco	tumbako	traffic	trefiki
today	leo	trail (route)	njia

train	treni/reli
train station	stesheni ya treni
translate	-tafsiri
to travel	-safiri
travel sickness	kutapika kwa ajili ya safari
travel books	vitabu vya usafiri
traveller	msafiri
travellers cheques	cheki za kusafiri
tree	mti
trendy	ya kisasa
trip	safari
trousers	suruali
truck	lori
true	kweli/hakika
	It's true.
	Ni kweli.
to trust	-amini
to try	-jaribu; -jitahidi; -fanya bidii
T-shirt	tishati
tune	wimbo
	Turn left.
	Pita kushoto.
	Turn right.
	Pita kulia.
TV	televisheni
twice	mara mbili
twin beds	vitanda viwili
twin	pacha (pl mapacha)
to type	-taipu

U

umbrella	mwavuli
uncomfortable	bila raha; bila starehe
under	chini; chini ya
underpants	chupi
to understand	-fahamu/ -elewa
	Do you understand?
	Unaelewa?/Unafahamu?
	I understand.
	Naelewa/Nafahamu.
	I don't understand.
	Sielewi/Sifahamu.
unemployed	asiye na kazi; lofa
union	ushirika/ chama
universe	ulimwengu
university	chuo kikuu
unsafe	si salama; ya hatari
until	mpaka/ hadi
unusual	siyo kawaida
up	juu/zaidi
upstairs	juu
urgent	muhimu sana
useful	inatumika

V

vacant	nafasi ipo
vacation	likizo/ livu
vaccination	chanjo
valley	bonde
Rift Valley	bonde la ufa
valuable	ya thamani
value (price)	bei/ thamani
vegetable	mboga
	I'm vegetarian.
	Mimi sili nyama.

vegetation	miti na mashamba
vein	mshipa
venereal disease	ugonjwa wa usharti
very	sana/ mno/ kabisa
video tape	kideo (pl video)
view	mandhari
village	kijiji
virus	kirus (pl virus)
visa	visa
to visit	-tembelea/ -zuru
vitamins	vitamini
voice	sauti
volume	sauti

Please turn down the volume!
Naomba upunguze sauti!

to vomit	-tapika
vote	kura
to vote	-piga kura

W

to wait	-ongoja/ -subiri

Wait!
Subiri!

waiter	mtumishi/ weita
to walk	-tembea
wall	ukuta
want (v)	-taka

I want …
Nataka …
Do you want …?
Unataka …?

war	vita

warm	joto kidogo
to wash (hands and face)	-nawa
to wash (clothes)	-fua
to wash (oneself)	-oga
to wash (things)	osha
watch	saa ya mkono
to watch	-tazama
water	maji
boiled water	maji ya moto
bottled water	maji ya chupa
waterfall	mporomoko wa maji
water purification tablets	vidonge vya kusafisha maji
way	njia/ namna/ jinsi

Please tell me the way to …
Tafadhali niambie njia kwenda …
Which way?
Njia gani?

we	sisi
weak	dhaifu/ goigoi
wealthy	tajiri
to wear	-vaa
weather	hali ya hewa
wedding	arusi/ harusi
wedding cake	keki
wedding present	zawadi ya harusi
week	wiki
this week	wiki hii
weekend	wikendi
to weigh	-pima

188

weight	uzito	wide	pana
welcome	karibu/	wife	bibi/
	karibuni		mke/
well (adj)	vizuri		mwanamke
well (n)	kisima	wild animal	mnyama porini
west	magharibi	to win	-shinda/
wet	-enye maji;		-faulu
	majimaji	wind	upepo
what	nini/	window	dirisha
	gani	wine	mvinyo

What's he saying?
Anasemaje?

		wings	mabawa
		winner	mshindaji

What's this?
Hii ni nini?

		wire	uzi wa madini
		wisdom	busara/
			akili/

What's this made of?
Hii imetengenezwa na nini?

			hekima

What time is it?
Ni saa ngapi?

		to wish	-ombi
when	lini;	with	na;
	wakati gani		pamoja na

When will the ... leave?
... itaondoka saa ngapi/lini?

		within	katika/
			ndani
where	wapi	without	bila

Where's the ...?
... iko wapi?

		woman	mwanmke

Where are the toilets?
Choo kiko sehemu gani?

			(pl wanawake)
white	-eupi	wonderful	ya ajabu
who	nani	wood	mbao
		wool	sufu

Who is it?/Who are they?
Ni nani?

		word	neno
		work	kazi

Who should I ask?
Nimuulize nani?

		to work	-fanya kazi
		work permit	ruhusa ya
whole	nzima/		kufanya kazi
	yote	workshop	warsha
		world	dunia/
why	kwa nini;		ulimwengu
	kwa sababu		
	gani;	to worry	-wa na
	mbona		wasiwasi

Why is the bank closed?
Kwa nini benki imefungwa?

Don't worry.
Usie na wasiwasi.

		worse	mbaya zaidi
		to worship	-sali

to write   -andika
writer   mwandishi
wrong   mbaya;
                -enye makosa

I'm wrong.
Nimekosa.

Y

year   mwaka
    years ago
    miaka iliyopita;
    miaka ya zamani
    this year
    mwaka huu
yellow   manjano
yellow fever   homa ya
                manjano
yesterday   jana
yesterday   jana mchana
    afternoon
yesterday   jana jioni
    evening
yesterday   jana asubuhi
    morning
yet   bado
young   ndogo
youth   kijana
                (pl vijana)

Z

zebra   punda milia

Most verbs and many adjectives are shown in their stem form – i.e., stripped of any of the prefixes that describe the action of the verb or the subject of the adjective. For a detailed explanation, read through the relevant sections on page 22 in the Grammar chapter. Many words that are adjectives in English are adjectival phrases in Swahili; for example, the literal translation of -enye baridi kidogo which we use for 'cool', is 'with a little cold'.

When you see the word -enye or -a, refer to the following chart for the correct form to use in 'survival' Swahili sentences:

one person	mwenye	wa
two (or more) people	wenye	wa
one thing	yenye	ya
two (or more) things	zenye	za

A

abiria	passenger
-acha	to quit
ada	fee
adhabu	correction
-adhibu	to punish
adimu	rare
afadhali	preferable
afisa	officer
afisi	office
afya	health
Afya, Mungu akubariki.	
Bless you. (when sneezing)	
-agiza	to order
agizo	order (n)
ahadi	promise (n)
-ahidi	to promise
aibu	embarrassment/ shyness
aina	brand/ kind
aina ya damu	blood type

ajabu	surprise (n)
ya ajabu	amazing/ marvellous/ strange
ajali	accident
-ajiri	to hire
akili	imagination/ intelligence/ mind/wisdom
akina babu	ancestors
alama	sign (symbol)
alfajiri	dawn
-alika	to invite
aliyeshindwa	loser
ama	or
amani	peace
-ambia	to tell
ambukizo	infection
amekufa	dead
Amekufa.	
She/he is dead.	

-amini — to believe/trust
-amua — to decide
anasa — luxury
-andaa — to prepare food
chakula
andamano — procession
-andika — to write
-angalia — to look at
Angalia! — Careful!
Uwe mwangalifu! — Be careful!
angalifu — careful
angavu — bright
anwani — address
-anza — to begin/start
ardhi — earth (soil)/land
mtelemko wa ardhi — landslide
arusi — wedding
asali — honey
Asante. — Thank you.
asilimia ... — ... percent
(mali) asili — natural resources
(ya) asili — original
asiye na kazi — unemployed
asubuhi — morning
jana asubuhi — yesterday morning
au — or
-azima — to borrow

B

baa — bar
baada ya siku (sita) — in (six) days
baadaye — after(wards)/later
Baadaye. — See you later.
baadhi — some

baba — dad/father
baba watoto — husband
babamkwe — father-in-law
babu — grandfather
-badili/ — to exchange
-badilisha
-badili pesa — to change money
bado — not yet/yet
bafu — bath/shower
bafuni — bathroom (shower)
bahari — ocean/sea
urefu juu ya bahari — altitude
bahasha — envelope/parcel
bahati — chance/luck
Bahati njema! — Good luck!
-bahatisha — to guess
baina ya — among
-baini — to recognise
baisikeli — bicycle
baisikeli kwenye gia — mountain bike
-baki — to be left (behind, over); to stay (remain)
bakshishi — tip (gratuity)
balozi — ambassador
-bana — (to be) tight
bandari — harbour/port
banghi — dope (marijuana)/pot
bangili — bracelet
barabara (kuu) — (main) road
barafu — ice
baraza — balcony
baridi — cold (temp)
maji baridi — cold water
Ni baridi. — It's cold.
ya baridi — chilled
-bariki — to bless

barua — letter/mail
basi — bus/ coach
  basi inayofuata
  next bus
  basi ya kusafiri mbali
  long-distance bus
-beba — to carry
bega — shoulder
begi — handbag
bei rahisi — cheap
bei — cost/price/value
  Je, unaweza kupunguza bei?
  Can you lower the price?
  Kiasi gani?
  How much?
  Ni bei gani?
  How much (does it cost)?
  Ni bei gani mpaka ...?
  How much to ...?
-bembeleza — to cuddle
bendera — flag
bendi — band (music)
benki — bank
Bi — Mrs
biashara — business/ occupation
bibi — grandmother/ wife
Biblia — the Bible
-bichi — raw
bik — pen
bila — without
  bila mahali; bila nyumba — homeless
bila raha — uncomfortable
bila sauti — mute
bila starehe — uncomfortable
bilauri (ya maji) — glass (of water)
bima — insurance
  -fanya bima ya
  to insure

Ina bima.
It's insured.
Nina bima ya afya/usafiri.
I have health/travel insurance.
bin — descendant
binafsi — personal/private
  hospitali binafsi
  private hospital
binamu — cousin
binti — daughter
-bishi — to argue
biskuti — biscuit
boksi — box
bomba — pipe/ pump (water)
bomu — bomb
Bonde la Ufa — Rift Valley
bonde — valley
bora — better
boti — boat
buluu — blue
bunge — parliament
bure — free (of charge)
busara — intelligence/ mind/wisdom
bustani — garden/park
busu — kiss (n)
buti ya ku-pandia milima — hiking boots
bwana — husband
Bwana — Mr
bwawa (ya kuogolea) — swimming pool
-bweka — to bark

C

chache — few
-chache — little (amount)
chache zaidi — less
chafu — dirty
-chagua — to choose

chai cha asubuhi — breakfast

chakula — food

chakula cha mchana — lunch

chakula cha mdogo — baby food

chakula cha usiku — dinner

Karibu chakula! — Bon appétit!

sumu ya chakula — food poisoning

chama — organisation/(political) party/union

chandarua — net (mosquito net)

-changa/-changanya — to mix

chanjo — vaccination

chawa — lice

-cheka — to laugh

cheki za kusafiri — travellers cheques

cheko — laugh (n)

-chelewa — to be late

-chelewesha — to delay

Tulicheleweshwa. — We were delayed.

-chemsha — to boil

chenji — change/coins

-chenji — to change money

cheti — certificate

cheti cha kuzaliwa — birth certificate

cheti cha ruhusa — permit

cheti cha usafiri — boarding pass

-cheza — to play

-cheza densi — to dance

-cheza karata — to play cards

chifu — chief

chini — below/bottom/downstairs/low

chini (ya) — under

-choka — to be bored/tired

-choka sana — to be exhausted

-choma — to burn

choo — bathroom (toilet)

Choo kiko sehemu gani? — Where are the toilets?

Choo kiko wapi? — Where are the toilets?

karatasi ya choo — toilet paper

chubuko — bruise

-chukia — to hate

-chukiza — to offend

-chukua — to take/pick up

-chukuwa — to catch

chuma — metal

-chuma kwa kazi — to earn

chumba — room

chumba cha mtu moja — single room

chumba cha watu wawili — double room

Chumba hiki si kisafi. — This room isn't clean.

chumba kwenye AC — air-conditioned room

chumo — earnings

chumvi — salt

chungu — bitter; pot (ceramic)

chungwa — orange (fruit)

chuo kikuu — college/university

chupa — bottle

maji ya chupa — bottled water

chupi — underpants

D

dada	sister
dafu	coconut (fruit)
daima	permanent
dakika	minute

baada ya dakika (tano)
in (five) minutes
Nipe dakika moja.
Just a minute.

daktari	doctor
daktari wa meno	dentist
daladala	(Tanz) small bus
dalili	sign (symbol)
damu	blood

aina ya damu
blood type
shimikizo la damu
blood pressure
-toka damu
to bleed

-dang'anya	to cheat

Umenidang'anya!
You cheated me!

daraja	bridge
daraja la pili	second class
daraja la tatu	third class
daraka	responsibility
darasa	class (school)
darubini	binoculars
daraja	bridge
dawa	drugs/medicine

-lewa kwa dawa
to be stoned (drugged)

dawa ya kichwa	aspirin
dawa ya kufu-kuza wadudu	insect repellent
dawa ya kukinga jua	sunscreen/suntan lotion
dawa ya kulevya	drugs (illicit)
dawa ya kuondoa uchafu wa kuam-bukiza ugonjwa	disinfectant
dawa ya maumivu	painkillers
dawa ya meno	toothpaste
dawa ya sindano	injection
dawa ya vijidudu	antiseptic
dhahabu	gold
dhahiri	obvious
dhaifu	fragile/weak
dhambi	sin
-dhani	to think

Sidhani.
I don't think so.

dharuba	storm
dikteta	dictatorship
dini	religion
dira	compass
dirisha	window
dobi	laundry woman/man
-dogo	little/short/small
dogo zaidi	less
duara	round
duka	shop

Duka limefungwa.
The store's closed.

duka la dawa	chemist/pharmacy
duka la mkate	bakery
duka la nguo	clothing store
duka la vitabu	bookshop
dunia	the Earth/world

E

-egemea	to be/lean against
-elekeza	to direct
-elewa	to understand

Naelewa.
I see/understand.

Sielewi.
I don't understand.
Unaelewa?
Do you understand?
elimu education
-ema good
-enda to depart/go
  Endelea moja kwa moja.
  Go straight ahead.
  Nakwenda …
  I'm going to …
  Twende.
  Let's go.
-enda mudukani to shop
-endesha to drive/
  to have diarrhoea
Endesha Slow down!
polepole! (to a driver)
-endesha to cycle
  baisikeli
-endesha to push
  mbiyo
-enye akili sensible
-enye bahati lucky
-enye baridi cool (weather)
  kidogo
-enye busara sensible
-enye dhambi guilty
-enye furaha happy
-enye huruma kind
-enye kelele noisy
-enye kichaa crazy
-enye kuam- contagious
  bukiza
-enye kufun- open (adj)
  guliwa
-enye maji wet
-enye makosa wrong
-enye nguvu strong
-enye uhuru free (not bound)
-enye watu crowded
  wengi
-epesi quick

-eupe light (clear)
-eupi white
-eusi black

F

-fa to die
  Nitakufa tukiendelea.
  I'll die if we keep going.
fahali bull
-fahamiana to meet for the
  first time
-fahamu to know (s'one)/
  to understand
  Nafahamu.
  I understand.
  Sifahamu.
  I don't understand.
  Unafahamu?
  Do you understand?
fahari pride
faida advantage/profit
-fanana to be similar
-fanya to do
  Sijafanya.
  I didn't do it.
  Unafanyaje?
  What are you doing?
-fanya bidii to try
-fanya buking to book/reserve
-fanya kazi to work
-fanywa na made (to be
  made of)
farasi horse
-fariki to die
  (Mtoto) amefariki.
  (Our child) died.
  Amefariki dunia.
  She/he has left this world.
-faulu to succeed/win
fedha money/silver
  mshika fedha
  cashier

feni	fan
-fika	to arrive/ to orgasm
fikara	idea/thought
-fikiri	to think
fikra	thought/mind
filamu ya sinema	film (movie)
filamu	cinema/movies
forodha	customs (border)
foronya	pillowcase
friji	refrigerator
-fua	to wash (clothes)
-fuata	to follow
fukara	poor
fukuzo	persecution
fulani	somebody
fundi	craftsman/ mechanic
-fundisha	to teach

Nifundishe.
Teach me.

-funga	to close/lock/ shut
-funga gerezani	to imprison
-funga tumbo	to be constipated
-fungua	to open

Watafungua saa ngapi?
What time does it open?

fupi	short (height)
-furaha	to have fun
-furahi	to be happy
-furahia	to enjoy
-furahisha	to please
furiko la maji	flood
furushi	package

G

-ganda	to freeze
gani	what

Kiasi gani?
How much?

Ni bei gani?
How much (does it cost)?
Ni bei gani mpaka ...?
How much to ...?

gari	car
mafuta ya gari	motor oil
gari la moshi	railroad
gawa	to share
gazeti	magazine
gazeti (pl magazeti)	newspaper
gelasi (ya maji)	glass (of water)
-geni	exotic
gereza	jail/prison
gesti	(cheap) hotel
ghafla	emergency/ suddenly
kwa ghafla	instant
ghali	expensive
gharika	flood
ghorofa	floor (storey)
ghuba	bay
giza	dark
globu	light bulb
godoro	mattress
goigoi	weak
-gombana	to fight/quarrel
gome	shell
goti	knee
-piga goti	to kneel
gramu	gram
gumu	difficult/hard/ solid
kichwa ngumu	stubborn
-gundua	to discover
-gusa	to touch

H

habari	information/news

Habari!
Hello!

Habari za asubuhi.
  Good morning.
Habari za jioni.
  Good evening.
Habari za mchana.
  Good afternoon.
habari yote   detail
habari za   current affairs
  kisasa
hadi   until
hadithi   story/tale
haieleweki   incomprehensible
haiwezikani   impossible
  Haiwezikani.
  It's impossible.
haki   justice
  Una haki.   You're right.
  ya haki   legal
haki ya uraia   civil rights
(ya) hakika   certain/sure/true
-hakikisha   to confirm
hakimu   judge
halali   legal
hali   situation
  hali ya maisha
  standard of living
hali ya hewa   atmosphere/
  temperature/
  weather
hali ya kutapika   nausea
halili   perfect/pure
halisi   pure
hamu ya   homesick
  kurudi nyumbani
-hangaikia   to suffer
hapa   here
  papa hapa   immediately
  Simama hapa.
  Stop here.
hapo   there
haraka   fast (quick)
  kwa haraka   in a hurry

harakati   process
-harakisha   to be in a hurry
-haribu   to corrupt/destroy
-harisha   to have diarrhoea
  Naharisha.
  I've got diarrhoea.
harufu   smell (n)
harusi   wedding
hasara   disadvantage
hashishi   dope
hata milele   forever
hata moja   none
hatari   danger/risk
  ya hatari   dangerous
haya   OK
haya   embarrassment/
  shyness
hekima   wisdom
hela   money
hema   tent
  -piga hema   to camp
hereni   earrings
  Heri na hongera!
  Many happy returns!
  Heri za sikukuu.
  Happy birthday. (lit: blessings
  on your holiday)
-hesabu   to count
heshima   respect
heshimiwa   respected person
hewa   air/oxygen/sky
hifadhi   park
-hifadhi   to take care of/
  to protect
hifadhi ya   protected forest
  misitu
himiza   push
-hisi   to feel
-hitaji   to need
hivi   approximately
hivi karibuni   recently
homa   fever

homa ya manjano	yellow fever
hongera	congratulations
hospitali binafsi	private hospital
hotuba	political speech
huduma ya kwanza	first-aid
huduma	service (help)
huenda	probably
huko	there
humo	there
huru	free (not bound)
huzuni	sadness

I

-iba	to rob/steal
	Niliibiwa!
	I was robbed!
Ijumaa	Friday
ikiwa	if
ile ile	same
(nusu saa) iliopita	(half an hour) ago
imara	solid
-imba	to sing
imejaa	full (it is full)
-inama	to bend
Inatosha!	Enough!
inatumika	useful
inayobaki	rest (remainder)
-ingi	many
-ingia	to enter
-ingine	another
injini	engine
-ishi	to live
isiyo ya rasmi	informal
isiyofaa	inconvenient
-ita	to call

J

-ja	to come
-jali	to care (about)
jamaa	family/relation
jambo	something
jambo la kubahatisha/ kujihatarisha	adventure
jamhuri	republic
jamii	society
ya jamii	public
jana	yesterday
	jana asubuhi
	yesterday morning
	jana jioni
	yesterday evening
	jana mchana
	yesterday afternoon
	jana usiku
	last night
jangwa	desert
janja	clever
-jaribu	to test/try
-jaza	to fill
jehenamu	hell
jela	prison
-jenga	to build
jengo	building
jeraha	injury
jeshi	military
jibu	to answer/answer(n)
jicho (pl macho)	eye
jifunza	learn
	Najifunza Kiswahili.
	I'm learning Swahili.
-jifurahisha	to enjoy (oneself)
-jikinga	to have safe sex
jiko	kitchen
jina	name
jina la kudangwa	nickname

jina la pili surname
Jina lako nani?
What's your name?
Jina langu ni ...
My name is ...
jino (pl meno) tooth
maumivu ya jino toothache
jinsi way/style
jioni evening
jana jioni
yesterday evening
jirani near
-jitahidi to try
-jiuzulu to resign
jiwe stone
jiwe (pl mawe) rock
johari jewel
joto heat/hot
Ni joto.
It's hot.
joto kidogo warm
jozi pair
-jua to know (s'thing)
Sijui.
I don't know.
jua sun
Kuna jua.
It's sunny.
Jumamosi Saturday
jumla together
jusi juice
-juta to regret
juu high/over/
up/upstairs
kwenda juu to climb
juu ya about/above/
on/over
juzi day before
yesterday

K

kaa crab
-kaa to live/stay
(somewhere);
to sit
kabati cupboard
kabeji cabbage
kabisa absolutely/
totally/
very
mbaya kabisa terrible
kabla ya before
kaburi cemetery/grave
kadhaa several
-kagua to check
kahaba prostitute
kahawa coffee
kaka brother
kalamu pen/pencil
kale ancient
ya kale old
kama approximately/as/
if/like (similar)
kamba rope/seatbelt
kamili exactly/perfect
kamusi dictionary
kamwe never
kanda cassette
kanda recording (music)
(ya musiki)
kanisa church
kanisa ya synagogue
kiyahudi
kanuni rule (n)/
standard (adj)
kaptura shorts
karamu festival/
party
karani secretary
karantini quarantine
karata playing cards

karatasi	paper
karatasi ya choo	
toilet paper	
-karibisha	to invite
karibu	almost/close/near/soon
karibu(ni)	welcome
Karibu chakula!	
Bon appétit!	
karibu na	by
karimu	generous/kind
kaskazini	north
kata	to cut
-kata	to chop
-kataa	to refuse
-kata shauri	to decide
-kataza	to deny
(ya) kati ya mataifa	international
katibu	secretary
katika	among/at/during/in/within
katikati	between/centre
kati ya	among
-kauka	to dry
kata	to cut
kavu	arid/dry
(ya) kawaida	common/ordinary/standard
kazi	job/occupation/work
kazi ofisini	
office work	
kazi ya mikono	
handicrafts	
kazi ya mkono	
manual work	
kazi ya nyumbani	
housework	
keki	wedding cake
kelele	noise
-piga kelele	to shout

kemra	camera
kengele	bell
kesho	tomorrow
kesho asubuhi	
tomorrow morning	
kesho jioni	
tomorrow evening	
kesho kutwa	
day after tomorrow	
kesho mchana	
tomorrow afternoon	
-keti	to sit
kiasi	approximately/a little bit/size
Can you lower the price?	
Kiasi gani?	
kiatu (pl viatu)	shoe
kibao	sign (posting)
kibinadamu	human
kibiriti (pl vibiriti)	match
kichaa	mad/maniac
kichanuo	comb/hairbrush
kicheko	laugh (n)
kichwa	head
kichwa ngumu	stubborn
kideo (pl video)	video tape
kidogo	small
kidole (pl vidole)	finger
-onyesha (wa kidole)	
to point (with finger)	
kidonge (pl vidonge)	pill
vidonge vya kusafisha maji	
water purification tablets	
kidonge cha kuzuia mimba	
the Pill	
kienyeji	local
kifafa	epilepsy
kifiko	destination
kifo	death

kifuli	bottle opener/lock
kifundofundo	epilepsy
kifungo	imprisonment/ prison/ prison sentence
kifunguo cha kopo/mkebe	tin/can-opener
kufungwa	imprisonment
kifurushi	parcel
(ya) kigeni	foreign/ strange
Kiingereza	English (language)

Je, unasema Kiingereza?
Do you speak English?

kijana (pl vijana)	youth
kijeshi	military
kijiji	village
kijiji jirani ya mji	suburb
kikapu	basket
(ya) kike	female (gender)
kikohozi	cough (n)
kikombe	cup
kikundi	band (music)
kila	each/every
kila kitu	detail/everything
kila mtu	everyone
kila mwaka	annual
kila siku	daily
kila wakati	always
kile kile	same
kilele	peak
kilema	disabled/ paraplegic
kilima	hill
kilimo	agriculture
kilio	funeral
kilo	kilogram
kimo	altitude
kimya	mute/quiet
kina	depth

kinyume cha sheria	illegal
kinyume	opposite
kinywaji	drink (n)
kioo	mirror
kioo cha taa ya umeme	light bulb
kipaka	kitten
kipande	part/piece
kipepeo	butterfly
kipindi	short (time)
kiplefti	roundabout
kipofu	blind
-kiri	to confess
kiroboto	flea
kirus (pl virus)	virus
(ya) kisasa	present (adj)/ modern/ trendy
-kimbia	to run
kisi	kiss
kisima	well (n)
kisiwa	island
kisu	knife
Kiswahili	Swahili

Nasoma Kiswahili.
I'm learning Swahili.
Nasema Kiswahili.
I can speak Swahili.
Sisemi Kiswahili.
I can't speak Swahili.

kitabu (pl vitabu)	book

kitabu cha hadithi
novel (book)
kitabu cha mwongozo/ maelezo
guidebook
kitabu kwenye namba za simu
telephone book
vitabu vya usafiri
travel books

kitambaa — bandage/cloth/material

kitambulisho — ID (card)

kitanda — bed

  kitanda cha watu wawili
  double bed

  vitanda viwili
  twin beds

kiti — chair/seat

kitu — something

  Siyo kitu.
  It doesn't matter.

kitu chochote — anything

kituo — stop (n)

kituo cha basi — bus stop

kitunga — basket

(ya) kiume — male (gender)

kivuli — shade/shadow

kiwanda — factory/industry

kiwanja cha ndege — airport

kiziwi — deaf (person)

kizuio — checkpoint

kizunguzungu — dizzy

kodi — rent/tax

kodi ya mapato — income tax

-kodi — to rent

-kohowa — to cough

kompyuta — computer

kona — corner

kondakta — conductor

kondom — condom

kondoo — sheep

koo — throat

kopo — can/

  ya kopo — tin canned

kosa (langu) — (my) fault/mistake

-kosa — to miss (eg bus)/to lose (s'thing)

kosefu — guilty

koti — coat/overcoat

kriket — lighter

Krismasi — Christmas

(ya) kuambukiza — infectious

kubadili treni — change (trains)

-kubali — to accept/to admit/to agree

  Sikubali.
  I don't agree.

  Tunakubaliana!
  Agreed! (we agree)

kubwa — big/large

kucha — dawn

(ya) kuchekesha — funny

kuchomwa na jua — sunburn

(ya) kuchosha — boring

(ya) kufaa — practical

(ya) kufuata — next

kufuli — padlock

(ya) kufurahisha sana — delightful

kuhusu — about

kuingiza vitu kutoka nchi za nje — to import

(ya) kukaangwa — fried

kuku — chicken

kule — there

kulia — right (not left)

  Pita kulia.
  Turn right.

-kumbatiana — to hug

-kumbuka — to miss (feel absence of)/to remember

kumbukumbu — diary/souvenir

nguzo ya kumbukumbu — monument

kuna mawingo — cloudy

ya kung'aa — bright

kunguni — bedbug
kuni — firewood
kupanda milima — mountaineering
(ya) kupendeza — pretty/interesting
Unapendeza!
You look pretty!
(ya) kupendeza sana — delightful
kupendezwa — to be interested
kura — vote
-piga kura — to elect/vote
-kusaidia — to aid
kushoto — left (not right)
Pita kushoto.
Turn left.
kusini — south
kusoma — learn
Nasoma Kiswahili.
I'm learning Swahili.
-kuta — find
-kuta (na) — to meet
Nitakukuta na.
I'll meet you.
kutapika kwa ajili ya safari — travel sickness
kutapika wakati wa usafiri — seasick
kutoka — from
(ya) kutosha — enough
(ya) kutumika — practical
(ya) kuumiza — painful
(ya) kuvunjikaupesi — fragile
(ya) kuvuta — interesting
kuvutiwa — to be interested
kuwa — to be
kwa kuwa — for
kuwa na — to have
Nina ...
I have ...

Una ...
You have ...
Una ...?
Do you have ...?
kuwa na uwoga — to be afraid
kuzuwia mimba — contraceptive
kwa — at/by/during/for/in/toward
kwa ghafla — instant
kwa haraka — in a hurry
Kwa heri.
Goodbye.
kwa kuwa — for
kwa meli — surface mail (by boat)
kwa mfano — for example
kwa milele — forever
kwa ndege — air mail
kwa nini — why
Kwa nini benki imefungwa?
Why is the bank closed?
kwa sababu — because
kwa sababu gani — why
kwa sababu ya — since (because)
kwa sauti kubwa — loud
-kwama/-kwamisha — to be stuck
kwangu — home
kwanza — first
huduma ya kwanza — first-aid
komunio ya kwanza — communion
kweli — true
Ni kweli.
It's true.
kwenda juu — to scale (climb)

L

kwenda mwezini — menstruation
  maumivu ya kwenda mwezini
  menstrual pains
kwenda na — round trip
  kurudi
kwenye — aboard (a boat/
  (ndege/meli) — plane)
kwenye — toward
  upande wa
kwetu — home

L

-la — to eat
  Umekula tayari?
  Have you eaten yet?
labda — maybe/probably
ladha (nzuri) — tasty
laiseni (ya — (driver's) licence
  kuendesha gari)
lakini — but
-lala; — to sleep
-lala usingizi
-lalana — to have sex
-laumu — to blame
lazima — necessary
lengelenge — blister
leo — today
leo usiku — tonight
-leta — to bring
-lewa — to be drunk
-lewa kwa — to be stoned
  dawa — (drugged)
-lia — to cry
likizo — holiday/vacation
-lima — to cultivate (land)
-linda — to protect
lini — when
  ... itaondoka saa ngapi/lini?
  When will the ... leave?
-lipa — to pay
livu — vacation

lofa — unemployed
lori — truck
lugha — language

M

maalum — particular/special
maamuzi — decision
(ya) maana — important/serious
  Siyo ya maana.
  It's not important.
maandamano — demonstration
  (protest)
maarifa — experience
maarifa ya — archaeology
  mambo ya kale
maarufu — famous
mabawa — wings
machela — hammock
macho — eyes
machozi — tears (crying)
maendeleo — development
mafanikio — success
mafua — cold (illness)
mafuatano — series
mafunzo — education
mafuta — fat/oil
mafuta — motor oil
  ya gari
mafuta — cooking oil
  ya kupikia
mafuta ya taa — lamp oil
magharibi — evening/sunset/
  west
maghofu — ruins
mahabusi — convict
mahadhi — rhythm
mahakama — court (law)
mahali — destination/
  location/place
mahali pa — accommodation
  kulalia

mahali pa kupiga hema — campsite

mahali pa kuzaliwa — place of birth

maharage (maharagwe) — beans

mahindi — corn/maize

mahojiano — interview

maisha — life

maji — water

  maji baridi — cold water

  maji ya chupa — bottled water

  maji ya kunywa — drinkable water

  maji ya moto — boiled water

  maji yaliosafishwa — filtered water

  mporomoko wa maji — waterfall

majimaji — wet

majivuno — pride

makao — homeland

(-enye) makosa — wrong

  Nimekosa. — I'm wrong.

maksusi — specific

maktaba — library

makumbusho — museum

malaya — prostitute

mali asili — natural resources

malipo — fee/payment

-maliza — to end

mama — mother

mamamkwe — mother-in-law

mamba — crocodile

mandamano — protest (n)

mandhari — view

manjano — yellow

homa ya manjano — yellow fever

maombi — petition

maongezi — conversation

maoni — opinion

maono — feelings

maonyesho — show (n)

maonyo — correction

mapato — profit

(Ni) mapema. (It's) early.

mapendekezo — proposal

mapenzi — romance

mapinduzi wa serikali — coup d'état

mapinduzi — revolution

mara kwa mara — sometimes

mara mbili — double/twice

mara moja — instant

mara moja tu — once

mara nyingi — often

mashariki — east/sunrise/west

mashine — machine

mashua — motorboat

maskini — poor

matatu — small local city bus (Kenya)

mateso — persecution

matokeo — results

maumivu — ache/cramp/injury/pains

maumivu ya jino — toothache

maumivu ya kwenda mwezini — menstrual pains

mauti — death

mavuno — produce (n)

mawazo — imagination

mawe — rocks

mawimbi — tide

mawingu — clouds

mazao	produce (n)
mazingira	environment
maziwa	milk
(ya) maziwa	dairy (products)
maziwa ya mtindi	cream
mazungumzo	conversation
mbaguzi wa jinsi	sexist
mbaguzi wa rangi	racist
(ya) mbali	apart/far/remote
Ni umbali gani ...? How far is ...?	
mbali mbali	different
mbao	board/wood
mbaya	bad/wrong
mbaya kabisa	terrible
mbaya sana	awful
mbaya zaidi	worse
mbele	ahead
mbele ya	in front of
mbeleni	future
mbingu	space (heavens)
mbinu	technique
mboga	vegetable
mbona	why
mbuga ya wanyama	national park
mbunge	Member of Parliament
mbuzi	goat
mbwa	dog
mbwa mdogo	puppy
mchana	afternoon
jana mchana	yesterday afternoon
mchana huu	this afternoon
mchanga	sand
mtoto mchanga	baby
mchezaji	player (sports)

mchezo (pl michezo)	game/sport
mchezo wa kuigiza	play (theatre)
mchongaji	sculptor
mchongo	sculpture
mchoraji	sculptor
mchoro	sculpture
mchumba	fiancé/e
mchungaji	minister
mdomo	mouth
mdudu	bug
-mea	to grow
meli	boat/ship
kwa meli	surface mail (by boat)
meli cha kuvushia watu	ferry
meno	teeth
meza	table
mfalme	king
mfano	example
kwa mfano	for example
mfanya- biashara	business person
mfanyakazi	employee
mfuko	bag/backpack
mfuko	pocket
mfululizo	series
mfungwa	convict/prisoner
mfupa	bone
mgahawa	cafe
mganga	doctor
mgeni	stranger
mgomo	a strike
mgongo	back (body)
mguu	foot/leg
mhogo	cassava
mhuni	creep (slang)
miaka	age
miaka iliyo- pita/ya zamani	years ago

midomo	lips
mila na desturi	customs (traditions)
(kwa) milele	forever
milioni	million
(kuwa na) mimba	pregnant (to be)
mimi	I
Mimi ni mgonjwa.	
I've got a cold.	
Mimi sijali.	
I don't care. (no problem)	
Mimi sili nyama	
I'm vegetarian.	
misa	mass/ religious service
misikiti	mosque
mita	metre
miti na mashamba	vegetation
miwani	glasses
miwani ya jua	sunglasses
mizigo	luggage
Mizigo	Baggage Claim
mjanja	crafty
mji	city/town
mji mkangwe	old city
kijiji jirani ya mji	suburb
mjinga	idiot
mjini	downtown
mjukuu	grandchild
mjumbe	representative
mjuzi wa ujenzi	architect
mkaa	charcoal
mkahawa	café/ restaurant
mkali	aggressive
mkanda ya kemra	film (roll of)
mkataba	contract
mkate	bread
mke	wife

mkebe	tin (can)
ya mkebe	canned
mkeka	mat
mkimbizi	refugee
mkoa	region
mkoba	handbag/town
mkono	arm/hand
kazi ya mikono	handicrafts
saa ya mkono	wristwatch
ya mikono	handmade
mkristu	Christian
mkufu	necklace
mkuku	spear
mkulima	farmer
mkutano	appointment
mkuu	chief/manager
mkuu wa polisi	chief of police
mlafi	greedy person
mlango	door/entry
mlango wa nje	gate
mle	there
mlevi	drunkard
mlima	mountain
mlima mkali	steep
mlio	cry (n)
mmea	plant (n)
mnene	fat person
mno	too (many/much); very
mnyama porini	wild animal
mnyama (pl wanyama)	animal
moja	one
Endelea moja kwa moja.	
Go straight ahead.	
moja kwa moja	direct/straight
mara moja	instant
mara moja tu	once

moshi	smoke/steam	mteja	client
mosi	one	mtelemko wa ardhi	landslide
moto	fire/heat/hot	mtengenezaji	editor
motokaa	car	mtetemeko wa nchi	earthquake
moyo	heart	mti	tree
mpaka	border/until	mtihani	test (n)
mpenzi	girl/boyfriend/lover	mtindo	style
mpiga picha	photographer	mto	pillow/river/stream
mpira	ball/chewing-gum/football	mtoto (pl watoto)	child
mpishi	cook (n)	mtoto mchanga	baby
mporomoko wa maji	waterfall	mtoto wa bandia	doll
mpumbavu	idiot/stupid person	mtoto wa kike	girl
mpya	new/modern	mtu	person
mradi	program	kila mtu	everyone
mradi wa msaada	aid organization	mtu moja	somebody
mrefu	tall	mtu mtamu/mwema	nice person
msaada	aid/help/service	mtu mzima	adult
msafiri	traveller	mtu wa dini	religious person
msalaba	cross (n)	mtumishi	waiter
msenge (n)	homosexual	mtungi	jar
mshahara	earnings/salary	muda	time
mshika fedha	cashier	muda mfupi	short (time)
mshindaji	winner	muhimu	important
mshipa	vein	Ni muhimu.	It's important.
mshumaa	candle	Siyo muhimu.	It's not important.
msibu	fortune teller	muhimu sana	urgent
msichana	girl	Muingereza	English person
mstari	line	mume	husband
mswaki	toothbrush	Mungu	God
mtaalamu	specialist	musuli	muscle
mtakatifu	saint	muziki	concert
mtalamu	professional	mvinyo	wine
mtalii	tourist	mviringo	circle/round
mtawala kwa nguvu peke yake	dictatorship		

mvua	rain

Mvua inanyesha.
It's raining.

mvulana	boy/son
mvumulivu	patient (adj)
mwajiri	employer
mwaka	year
kila mwaka	annual
mwaka huu	this year
mwaka uliyopita	last year
mwalimu	instructor/ teacher
mwamba	cliff
mwaminifu	honest
mwamuzi	referee
mwana sheria	lawyer
mwanachama	member
mwanafunzi	beginner/ student
mwanamke	female/wife
mwanamuziki	musician
mwananchi	citizen
mwanasanaa	artist
mwanasayansi	scientist
mwanasiasa	politician
mwanaume (pl wanaume)	man
mwandishi	writer
mwanga	light
mwanamke (pl wanawake)	woman
mwavuli	umbrella
mwembamba	thin
mwendo	speed

Punguza mwendo!
Slow down! (to a driver)

mwenye huruma	sympathetic
mwenye pumu	asthmatic
mwenye(we)	owner
mwenyekiti (wa kijiji)	mayor (of the village)
mwenyekiti	chairperson

mwenzake	his/her companion
mwenzako	your companion
mwenzangu	my companion
mwenzi	colleague
mwezi	month/moon
mwezi huu	this month
mwezi ujayo	next month
mwezi uliyopita	last month
mwigo	imitation
mwili	body
mwimbaji	singer
mwisho	end (n)
(ya) mwisho	last (adj)

Meli ya mwisho itaondoka saa ngapi?
What time does the last boat leave?

mwislamu	Muslim
mwizi (pl wezi)	thief
mwokaji (mikate)	baker
mwombaji	beggar
mwongo	liar
mwongozi	guide/leader
mwuguzi	nurse
mwuuza nyama	butcher
mzaha	joke (n)

Nafanya mzaha.
I'm joking.

mzee	old person (respected elder)
mzigo	suitcase
mzito	serious
Mzungu	European
mzuri	handsome

N

na	and/by/ with
nafasi ipo	vacant

nafasi — chance/opportunity/space (room)
-najisi — to rape
namna — way/style
namna gani — how
nani — who
  Ni nani?
  Who is it?/Who are they?
  Nimuulize nani?
  Who should I ask?
Naumwa kichwa.
I have a headache.
-nawa — to wash (hands and face)
nchi za nje — abroad/overseas
nchi — country/homeland
  mtetemeko wa nchi
  earthquake
  ya nchi nyingine
  foreign/strange
ndani — in/indoors/inside/within
ndani ya — inside
ndani ya nyumba — indoors
ndani yake — included
ndege — aeroplane/bird
  kampuni ya ndege — airline
  kwa ndege — air mail
  ndege yangu — my flight
ndevu — beard
ndizi — banana
ndoa — marriage
ndogo — young
ndoo — bucket
ndoto — dream (n)
ndugu — comrade/relation
nene — thick
-nenepa — to fatten
neno — word
nesi — nurse
ng'ambo — across

ng'ombe — cattle/cow
  ng'ombe dume — bull
ngazi — stairs
ngoma — dance (with traditional drums)
ngozi — leather/skin
nguo ya kuogolea — swimsuit
nguo — clothes
nguruwe — pig
nguvu — energy/power/strength
nguzo ya kumbukumbu — monument
ni rahisi — economical
  Niacha!
  Get lost!
  Niliibiwa!
  I was robbed!
  Nina njaa.
  I'm hungry.
nini — what
  Hii imetengenezwa na nini?
  What's this made of?
  Hii ni nini?
  What's this?
  kwa nini
  why
  Kwa nini benki imefungwa?
  Why is the bank closed?
  Nipe ...
  Give me ...
  Nitakufa tukiendelea.
  I'll die if we keep going.
  Nitakukuta na.
  I'll meet you.
nje — out/outside
  mlango wa nje — gate
njia — path/road/street/trail/process/way
  njia gani
  Njia gani?
  Which way?

Ni njia gani kufika ...?
How do you get to ...?
njia ya kupanda mlimani
mountain path
njia ya miguu
footpath
Njoo!
Come!

noti	banknote
-nuka	to smell (bad)
-nukia	to smell (good)
nukta	full stop (period)
-nunua	to buy
nusu	half

nusu saa iliopita
half an hour ago

nyama	meat

mwuuza nyama butcher
nyama ya ng'ombe beef

nyasi	grass
nyayo	track (footprints)
nyekundu	red
nyepesi	light (not heavy)
nyika	desert
nyingi	a lot

mara nyingi often

nyingine	other

ya nchi nyingine
foreign (of country)

-nyoa	to shave
-nyonyesha	to breastfeed
nyota	star
nyuma	back/behind

ya nyuma late

nyumba	house

bila nyumba homeless
ndani ya nyumba indoors
nyumba ya sanaa art gallery

nyumbani	home
nyundo	hammer
-nywa	to drink
nywele	hair
nzima	whole

nzuri	delicious/friendly
nzuri kabisa sana	best
nzuri zaidi	better

O

OB (brand name)	tampons
-oa	to marry (for a man)
ofisi ya tikiti	ticket office
-oga	to bathe
-ogolea	to swim
-ogopa	to fear
-okoa	to save
-okota	to pick up
-olewa	to marry (for a woman)
-omba lifti	to hitchhike
-ombi	to wish
-ona	to feel/see

Tutaonana.
Goodbye.
Tutaona!
We'll see!
Tutaonana kesho.
See you tomorrow.

-ona haya	to be shamed
-ona wivu	to be jealous
-ondoka	to depart/exit
-ongea	chat/talk
-ongoja	to wait
-ongoza	to guide
-ongoza	to direct
-onyesha	to exhibit/show

Nionyeshe.
Show me.
-onyesha (wa kidole)
to point
Unaweza kunionyesha
kwenye ramani?
Can you show me on the map?

orodha ya vyakula	menu
osha	to wash (things)

P

-pa	to give
Nipe ...	
Give me ...	
paa	roof
pacha	twin
(pl mapacha)	
padre	priest
paka	cat
-paka rangi	to paint
paki	to park a car
pale	there
pamba	cotton
pamoja	included/ together
Tupo pamoja.	
We're a couple.	
pamoja na	with
pana	wide
-panda	to ascend/board/ climb/plant
panga	sword
-panga	to hire/organise/ rent
pango	cave
panya	mouse/rat
papa hapa	immediately
-pasua	to break/destroy/ tear
-pata	to earn
-payuka	delirious
peke yake	alone/single (unique)
Ni peke yangu.	
I'm single.	
pekee	single (unique)
-peleka	to send
pembe	corner
pembeni	beside/next to
pembenne	square (shape)
-penda sana	to admire
-penda	to like
-penda	to love

Napenda/Sipendi ...	
I like/don't like ...	
Na(i)penda.	
I love it.	
Nakupenda.	
I love you.	
-pendana	to love each other
-pendekeza	to propose/ recommend
-pendelea	to prefer
pengine	maybe/ sometimes
peremende	sweet (candy)
pesa	money
pete	ring (on finger)
pia	also/too
picha	photo
piga chafya	sneeze
-piga goli	to score
-piga goti	to kneel
-piga hema	to camp
-piga kelele	to shout
-piga kura	to elect/ vote
-piga picha	to photograph
Naomba kupiga picha.	
May I take your photo?	
-piga risasi	to shoot
-piga simu	to telephone
Nitakupigia simu.	
I'll call you.	
-piga teke	to kick
-pigana	to fight
pigano	fight (n)
pigo	storm
-pika	to cook
pikipiki	motorcycle
(ya) pili	second (not first)
pilipili	pepper/ spicy
pima damu	blood test
-pima	to weigh
-pinda	to bend

Pita kulia.	Turn right.
Pita kushoto.	Turn left.
-pita	to pass
-pitia	to transmit
plasta	bandage
poda ya mtoto	baby powder
-pokea	to receive
Pole.	I'm sorry.
polepole	slow/slowly
pombe	beer
pombe kali	alcohol
-pona	to get better (from illness)
porini	bush country
posta	mail/post office
-posta	to ship
-potea	to be lost
-poteza	to lose (s'thing)
-potoa	to corrupt
-pumua	to breathe
-pumzika	to rest
pumziko	rest (relaxation)
punda milia	zebra
-punguza bei	to discount
Punguza mwendo!	Slow down! (to a driver)
-punja	to rip-off/chisel
pwani	beach/coast/seaside
-pya	new

R

rafiki	friend
raha	rest (relaxation)
rahisi	easy/simple
raia	citizen
rais	president
ramani	map
rangi	colour/race

mbaguzi wa rangi	racist
-paka rangi	to paint
rangi ya kahawa	brown
rangi ya machungwa	orange
rangi ya majani	green
rangi ya majivu	grey
rasimu	design
rasmi	formal
isiyo ya rasmi	informal
ratiba	calendar/itinerary/timetable
-refu	deep/high/long
-rejea	to return
reli	train
ripota	journalist
robo	a quarter
romani	Catholic
-rudi	to return
-rudia	to repeat
-rudisha pesa	to refund
ruhusa	permission
cheti cha ruhusa	permit (cert)
ruhusa ya kufanya kazi	work permit
ruhusa ya kuingia	admission
-ruhusu	to allow
Inaruhusiwa.	It's allowed.
-ruka	to fly/jump
rushwa	bribe/corruption
-toa rushwa	to corrupt

S

saa	clock/time
Ni saa ngapi?	What's the time?
nusu saa iliopita	half an hour ago
saa sita usiku	midnight

saa ya kuamsha **alarm clock**
saa ya mkono **wristwatch**
saa zote **always**
sababu **reason**
  kwa sababu **because**
  kwa sababu gani **why**
  kwa sababu ya **since (because)**
sabuni **soap**
safari **journey/trip**
safari ya kutalii **tour**
  Safari njema! **Bon voyage!**
safi **cool (slang)/good**
-safiri **to travel**
  cheki za kusafiri **travellers cheques**
-safisha **to clean**
sahani ya majivu **ashtray**
sahani **plate**
-sahau **to forget**
  Nimesahau. **I forget.**
sahihi **correct (adj)/signature**
-sahihisha **to correct**
-saidia **to help**
sakafu **floor**
sala **prayer**
salaidzi **slide film**
salama **safe/safety**
-sali **to worship**
-salimika **to survive**
samaki **fish**
-samehe **to forgive**
  Samehani! **Excuse me!**

sana **best/very**
  mbaya sana **awful**
  -penda sana **to admire**
sanaa **art/artwork/handicrafts**
sanamu **statue**
sanduku la posta (SLP) **mailbox (PO Box)**
sasa **now**
  (ya) sasa **fresh (not stale)**
  sasa hivi **immediately/right now**
sauti ya simu **dial tone**
sauti **sound/voice/volume**
  kwa sauti kubwa **loud**
  Naomba upunguze sauti! **Please turn down the volume!**
sawa **correct/equal/like (similar)/OK**
  Sawa. **Sure.**
  Sawa! **Agreed! (we agree)**
sawasawa **equal/same**
sayansi **science**
sayansi ya jamii **social science**
sayari **planet**
sefu **safe (n)**
sehemu **part/piece**
sekondari **high school**
selfon **mobile phone**
-sema **say/speak/talk**
  Anasemaje? **What is he saying?**
  Je, unasema Kiingereza? **Do you speak English?**
  Nasema Kiswahili. **I can speak Swahili.**
  Nasoma Kiswahili. **I'm learning Swahili.**

S

Sema polepole!	Slow down! (to someone speaking)
Sema tena.	(Could you) repeat that.
Sisemi Kiswahili.	I can't speak Swahili.
Unasemaje ...?	How do you say ...?
-sema uwongo	to lie
seminari	monastery
senti	cent
serikali	government
mapinduzi wa serikali	coup d'état
shahada	degree (univ)
shairi	poetry
shamba	farm/field
-shangaza	to surprise
Nashangaa.	I'm surprised.
shangazi	aunt (father's sister)
shati	shirt
shauri	advice
-kata shauri	to decide
-shauri	to advise
sherehe	party (n)
-sherehekea	to party
-sherekea	to celebrate
sheria	law/legislation/rule/statute
kinyume cha sheria	illegal
mwana sheria	lawyer
shida	problem
-shika	to catch
shilingi	money
shimikizo la damu	blood pressure
-shinda	to win
shindano	race (contest)
shindikizo	pressure
-shindwa	to lose (a game)

shirika	company/organisation
shiriki	to participate/to share
shoga	lesbian
-shona	to sew
shughuli	business/occupation
-shughulika	to be busy
shujaa	brave
shuka	sheet (bed)
shukrani	thanks
Shukrani.	Thank you.
-shukuru	to thank
shule	school
shule ya msingi	primary school
si kitu	nothing
si salama	unsafe
siafu	ant
siagi	butter
siasa	politics
sifa	quality
sifuri	none
sigara	cigarettes
-vuta sigara	to smoke cigarettes
-sikia	to hear/listen
-sikia kiu	to be thirsty
-sikia mgonjwa	to be ill
-sikia usingizi	to be sleepy
sikio (pl masikio)	ear
-sikitika	to be sad
siku	day
ya siku zote	permanent
kila siku	daily
siku tatu zilizopita	three days ago

216

T

siku hizi	modern/present (time)
siku kuu ya kuzaliwa	birthday
siku zijazo	future
sikukuu	festival/holiday
-simama	to stop
Simama hapa.	
Stop here.	
simbalis	guinea pig
simu	telephone (n)
Nitakupigia simu.	
I'll call you.	
-piga simu	
to telephone	
simu kutoka mbali/kutoka nchi ya nje	
long-distance/international call	
Sina ...	
I don't have ...	
sindano	syringe
sindano (ya dawa)	needle (syringe)
sindano (ya kushona)	needle (sewing)
sinema	cinema/movies
-sinzia	to sleep
siri	secret
sisi	we
siyo kawaida	unusual
Siyo kitu.	
It doesn't matter.	
Siyo muhimu.	
It's not important.	
slaisi	toast
soga	joke (n)
soka mpira	football
soko	market
-soma	to read
-staafu	to retire
-staajabu	to surprise
starehe	comfortable/luxury
-starehe	to relax
stempu	stamp
stendi	stop (bus)
stendi ya teksi	taxi stand
stesheni	station
-subiri	to wait
Subiri!	
Wait!	
sufu	wool
sufuria	pan
sukari	sugar
sukuma	push
-sumbua	to annoy
sumbufu	inconvenient/pain in the neck
sumu ya chakula	food poisoning
sumu ya mbu	coil (mosquito)
sungura	rabbit
sura ya nchi	scenery
sura	face
suruali	trousers
swali	question
sweta	jumper (sweater)

T

taa	lamp
mafuta ya taa	lamp oil
taabu	problem
taarifa	information/news
-tabasamu	to smile
Tabasamu!	
Smile!	
tafadhali	please
Tafadhali niambie njia kwenda ...	
Please tell me the way to ...	
Tafadhali, naweza kuazima ... yako?	
Please may I borrow your ...	
-tafsiri	translate

T

**D
I
C
T
I
O
N
A
R
Y**

-tafuta	to look for
Natafuta ...	
I'm looking for ...	
-taipu	to type
tajiri	rich/wealthy
-taka	to want
Nataka ...	
I want ...	
Nataka kuipanga.	
I want to hire it.	
Nataka kununua ...	
I'd like to buy ...	
Unataka ...?	
Do you want ...?	
takataka	garbage/rubbish
takatifu	holy
-tambua	to realise/ to recognise
tamu	delicious/sweet
tangu	from/since
-tania	to make fun of
-tapika	to vomit
taratibu	slow/slowly
tarehe	date (time)
tarehe ya kuzaliwa	date of birth
tatizo	problem
taulo	towel
-tawala	to rule
tawi	branch
tayari	already/ready
Tayari nimekula.	
I've already eaten.	
-tayarisha	to prepare
-tazama	to look at/watch
-teguka	to sprain
tele	plenty
-tembea	to stroll/walk
-tembea mlimani	to hike
-tembelea	to visit
tena	again/more/up
-tenga	to separate

-tengeneza	to make/ produce
-tenge- nezwa na	made (to be made of)
-teseka	to suffer
thamani	value (price)
ya thamani	valuable
tikiti	ticket
tikiti ya kwenda na kurudi	
return ticket	
tikiti ya kwenda tu	
one way ticket	
timu	team
tishati	T-shirt
titi	breast
-toa	to give/offer
-toa mimba	to have an abortion/ to miscarry
-toa rushwa	to corrupt
tofauti	different
Toka!	Get lost!
-toka damu	to bleed
-toka jasho	to perspire
tokea	from/since
tokeo	event
-tolea	tob offer
-tongoza	to date (s'one)
treni	railroad
tu	only
tukio	event
-tuma	to send
-tumaini	to hope
tumbako	tobacco
tumbo	stomach
tumbo linauma	
indigestion/stomachache	
tunda	fruit
-tunza	to take care of/ to protect
Tutaonana.	
Goodbye.	
Twende.	
Let's go.	

U

Swahili	English
ua (pl maua)	flower
-ua	to kill
ubaguzi	discrimination
ubaguzi wa rangi	racism
ubalozi	embassy
ubatizo	baptism
ubepari	capitalism
ubovu	corruption
uchafu	dirt/pollution
uchaguzi	election
uchaguzi wa vyama vingi	multi-party elections
uchumi	economy
udaktari wa kupasua	operation
udi	guitar
udongo	earth/dirt/mud
ufuasi	imitation
ufukara	poverty
ufukwe	beach
ufunguo	key
ufuoni	beach
ugomvi	quarrel
ugonjwa	cold (n)/disease/sickness
ugonjwa wa pumu	asthma
ugonjwa wa usharti	venereal disease
-ugua	to be ill
uhai	life
uhamiaji	immigration
uhusiano	relationship
uigaji	imitation
ujamaa	socialism
ujasiri	adventure
ujenzi	architecture/construction work
ujumbe	message
ujuzi	qualifications
ukapitalisti	capitalism
ukarimu	hospitality
ukimbioni	exile
ukimwi	AIDS
Ana kirus cha ukimwi.	She/he is HIV positive.
ukumbusho	souvenir
ukurasa	page/sheet (of paper)
ukurutu	itch/rash
ukuta	wall
ulimwengu	universe/world
uliopita	ago
muda uliopita	a while ago
-uliza	to ask
-uliza	to question
uma	hurt
-uma	to bite
umati wa watu	crowded
umaskini	poverty
umbo	shape
umeme	electricity
kioo cha taa ya umeme	light bulb
umimi	selfishness
umiza	hurt
umoja	equality
umri	age
-umwa	to be bitten/bitten
Unafahamu?	Do you understand?
unga	dust/flour
-ungama	to confess (relig)
unyevu	damp
upambanuzi	discrimination
upande	side
kwenye upande wa	toward
upele	itch/rash
upendo	love (n)
upepo	air/breeze/wind
upesi	fast/quick

upungufu	shortage
upungufu wa misitu	deforestation
uraia	citizenship/nationality
urefu juu ya bahari	altitude
usalama	safety
usawa	justice
ushirika	cooperative/union participation
ushirika wa wafanyakazi	trade union
ushuru	customs duty
ushuru wa usafiri	airport tax
Usijali.	Forget about it. (Don't worry.)
usiku	night
jana usiku	last night
leo usiku	tonight
saa sita usiku	midnight
usiku huu	tonight
usiku mpaka asubuhi	overnight
Usiku mwema.	Good night.
usingizi	sleep (n)
-lala usingizi	to sleep
-sikia usingizi	to be sleepy
uso	face
usoshalizm	socialism
usumbufu	harrassment
utawala	administration
utu	personality
uwanja	courtyard/square (town centre)
uwanja wa	stadium/sports field

uwezo wa kufanya kazi	energy
(ya) uwongo	false
-uza	to sell
-uza vitu nchi za nje	to export
uzi	string
uzi wa madini	wire
uzito	weight
uzoefu	experience
uzowevu wa ulevi	addiction

-vaa	to wear
-vaa kondom	to have safe sex
-vaa nguo	to dress
viatu	shoes
vidonge	pills/tablets
vifaa	equipment
vifungo	buttons
vipuli	jewelry
vita	fight/war
vitabu	books
vitanda	beds
vitu vya kale	antiques
vitu vya sanaa	crafts
vivu	lazy
vizuri	well (adj)
-vuka	to cross
-vuma	to blow
vumbi	dust
-vumbua	to discover
-vunjas	to break/destroy
-vunjika	to be broken
-vuta	to pull
-vuta (sigara)	to smoke (cigarettes)

W

-wa na haraka	to (be in a) hurry
-wa na kiu	to be thirsty
michezo	
-wa na njaa	to be hungry
Una njaa?	
Are you hungry?	
-wa na	to worry
wasiwasi	
Usie na wasiwasi.	
Don't worry.	
-wahi	to be early/to be on time
wakati	opportunity/time
kila wakati	always
wakati gani	when
wakati wa	during
wala	neither
waliowengi	majority
wanaofika	arrivals
Wanaoondoka	Departures
wao	they
wapi	where
... iko wapi?	
Where is the ...?	
warsha	workshop
wasenge	homosexuals
-washa	to itch/light (fire)
watu	people
ya watu wote	public
Wauzaje?	How much?
wazazi; wazee	parents
wazi	empty/obvious/ open
waziri mkuu	prime minister
wazo	idea/thought
-weka	to put
-weka akiba	to reserve
-weka sahihi	to sign
(ya) wema	friendly
wembe	razor
-weza	to be able (can)

Tunaweza kupiga hema hapa?	
Can we camp here?	
-wezekana	to be possible
-wia radhi	to forgive
wigo	fence
wiki	week
wiki hii	this week
wiki ijayo/kesho	
next week	
wiki jana/iliyopita	
last week	
wimbo	song/tune
(pl nyimbo)	
wingi	plenty
wingu	cloud
wote	together

Y

The word ya is used in combination with other words to form adjectives. They are listed here in their combined form under 'ya', and also appear in the vocabulary under the alphabetical listing of their main words.

ya ajabu	amazing/ marvelous/ strange/ wonderful
ya asili	original
ya baridi	chilled
ya haki	legal
ya hakika	positive (certain)
ya hatari	dangerous
ya jamii	public
ya kale	old
ya kati	international
ya mataifa	
ya kawaida	common/ ordinary/ standard

ya kigeni	foreign/strange	ya nyuma	late
ya kike	female (gender)	ya pili	second (not first)
ya kisasa	present (adj)/	ya pole	friendly
	modern/	ya sasa	fresh (not stale)
	trendy	ya siku zote	permanent
ya kiume	male (gender)	ya thamani	valuable
ya kopo	canned	ya uwongo	false
ya kuambukiza	infectious	ya watu wote	public
ya kuchekesha	funny	ya wema	friendly
ya kuchosha	boring	yaya	babysitter
ya kufaa	practical	yenye chumvi	salty
ya kufuata	next	yeye	she
ya kufura-	delightful	yote	all/whole
hisha sana		yote mbili	both
ya kukaangwa	fried	yoyote	any
ya kung'aa	bright	yule yule	same
ya kupendeza	pretty		

Unapendeza!
You look pretty!

ya kupendeza	interesting	zaidi	more/up
ya kupen-	delightful	mbaya zaidi	
deza sana		worse	
ya kutosha	enough	-zaliwa	to be born
ya kutumika	practical	zamani	past
ya kuumiza	painful	zamani sana;	long ago
ya kuvunjika	fragile	zamani za kale	
upesi		zambarua	purple
ya kuvuta	interesting	zao	crop
ya maana	important/	zawadi	present (gift)/tip
	serious	zawadi ya	wedding present
		harusi	

Siyo ya maana.
It's not important.

ya mbali	distant	-zee	old
ya mikono	handmade	-zidi kuishi	to survive
ya mkebe	canned	-zito	heavy
ya mwisho	last (adj)	ziwa	lake
		ziwi	deaf

Meli ya mwisho itaondoka
saa ngapi?
What time does the last boat
leave?

		-zuia	to prevent
		-zungumza	chat/talk
ya nchi	foreign	-zuri	beautiful/good/
nyingine			nice
		-zuru	to visit

CROSSWORD ANSWERS

Meeting People

Across
4. watoto
6. binti
7. habari

Down
1. mambo
2. karibu
3. hodi
5. kiu
6. bibi

Getting Around

Across
1. njia
3. ngapi
5. haraka
7. bima
8. kijiji

Down
1. ndege
2. anwani
4. pikipiki
6. mji

Accommodation

Across
3. simu
4. chakula
5. mto
6. dobi

Down
1. ufunguo
2. taa
3. sabuni
4. chumba

Shopping

Across
1. rahisi
3. kikoi
5. kanga
7. mswaki
8. zambarua

Down
2. inatosha
3. karatasi
4. kofia
8. nyuzi

In The Country

Across
3. shamba
4. fisi
7. sunguro
8. mamba

Down
1. buibui
2. mawingu
5. tumbili
6. pombe

INDEX